Unlocking Business Opportunities For Students

Asit Saha

Published by Asit Saha, 2024.

UNLOCKING BUSINESS OPPORTUNITIES FOR STUDENTS

First edition. March 30, 2024.

ISBN: 979-8224131075

Written by Asit Saha.

Overview

"Unlocking Business Opportunities for Students" is a comprehensive guide designed to empower students with the knowledge and tools needed to embark on entrepreneurial journeys while still pursuing their academic endeavors. This book serves as a roadmap for students eager to explore the world of business, providing practical advice, actionable strategies, and inspiring examples to help them navigate the complexities of entrepreneurship.

The overview begins by introducing the significance of entrepreneurship for students, emphasizing the value of developing entrepreneurial skills, mindset, and ventures early in life. It highlights the benefits of entrepreneurship, such as fostering creativity, problem-solving abilities, and financial independence, while dispelling common myths and misconceptions surrounding entrepreneurship.

Throughout the book, students are encouraged to identify their passions, skills, and interests, laying the foundation for discovering viable business opportunities aligned with their personal strengths. Various business models suitable for students are explored, ranging from e-commerce and freelancing to service-based ventures, accompanied by real-life examples illustrating each model's potential.

Students are guided through the process of conducting market research, refining business ideas, and developing comprehensive business plans tailored to their unique visions. Practical advice is offered on overcoming challenges commonly faced by student entrepreneurs, such as time management, balancing academic commitments, and navigating legal and ethical considerations.

"Unlocking Business Opportunities for Students" aims to equip students with the knowledge, confidence, and resources necessary to unleash their entrepreneurial potential, empowering them to create impactful ventures that drive innovation, solve societal challenges, and shape their future success.

Chapters

Chapter 1: Introduction

Chapter 1: Introduction

Welcome to "Unlocking Business Opportunities for Students," a guide crafted specifically for the dynamic minds of today's student entrepreneurs. In this book, we embark on a journey together, exploring the thrilling world of entrepreneurship tailored to the unique context of student life.

The purpose of this book is clear: to empower you, the student, with the knowledge, insights, and practical tools needed to unlock your entrepreneurial potential. Whether you're an aspiring entrepreneur with a budding idea or simply curious about the possibilities of business ownership, this guide is designed to be your trusted companion.

Entrepreneurship isn't just about commencing a businesses; it's about embracing a mindset of innovation, problem-solving, and resilience. As a student, you possess a wealth of untapped potential waiting to be unleashed. Through entrepreneurship, you have the opportunity to transform your passions, interests, and skills into meaningful ventures that not only enrich your life but also make a positive impact on the world around you.

In these pages, you'll find a treasure trove of practical advice, actionable strategies, and real-world examples to guide you through every step of your entrepreneurial journey. From identifying your passions and assessing market opportunities to developing business plans and overcoming challenges, each chapter is carefully crafted to provide you with the insights and tools you need to succeed.

Moreover, this book is not just about business; it's about personal growth and self-discovery. Along the way, you'll learn valuable lessons about resilience, adaptability, and the importance of embracing failure as a stepping stone to success. You'll be inspired by the stories of fellow student entrepreneurs who have defied the odds and turned their dreams into reality.

So, whether you're a student dreaming of launching your first startup or simply curious about the world of entrepreneurship, I invite you to dive into the pages of "Unlocking Business Opportunities for Students." Together, let's unlock your potential, seize new opportunities, and embark on a journey of discovery and growth. Welcome aboard!

Why exploring business opportunities as a student is valuable?

Exploring business opportunities as a student is immensely valuable for several compelling reasons:

Skill Development:

Engaging in entrepreneurial endeavors offers a unique opportunity for students to develop a wide range of practical skills that are highly sought after in today's job market. From critical thinking and problem-solving to communication and leadership, entrepreneurship offers a hands-on platform for honing these essential skills in a real-world context.

Innovation and Creativity:

Entrepreneurship encourages students to think outside the box, challenge the status quo, and innovate. By exploring business opportunities, students are empowered to unleash their creativity, generate new ideas, and develop innovative solutions to address existing challenges or meet unmet needs in society.

Financial Independence:

Starting a business as a student can provide a pathway to financial independence and self-sufficiency. Rather than relying solely on part-time jobs or financial assistance, entrepreneurship offers students the opportunity to create their own sources of income, build wealth, and gain financial stability early in life.

Networking and Relationship Building:

Entrepreneurship opens doors to valuable networking opportunities and allows students to connect with like-minded individuals, mentors, investors, and potential collaborators. Building a strong network of contacts not only facilitates the growth of their businesses but also lays the groundwork for future career opportunities and personal growth.

Hands-on Learning Experience: Entrepreneurship is a hands-on learning experience that complements traditional classroom education. By starting and running their own businesses, students gain practical insights into various aspects of business management, including marketing, finance, operations, and customer service, which are difficult to replicate in a classroom setting.

Empowerment and Self-Discovery: Entrepreneurship empowers students to take control of their futures, pursue their passions, and realize their full potential. Through the process of building and growing a business, students gain a deeper understanding of themselves, their strengths, and their values, fostering personal growth and self-discovery.

Generating Impact:

Entrepreneurship provides students with a platform to create meaningful impact in their communities and beyond. Whether by solving pressing social or environmental issues, supporting local economies, or inspiring others through their ventures, student entrepreneurs have the opportunity to make a positive difference in the world.

Chapter 2: Understanding Entrepreneurship for Students

Understanding entrepreneurship is crucial for students as it lays the foundation for their journey into the world of business and innovation. Here's why grasping the concept of entrepreneurship is essential:

Defining Entrepreneurship:

It's important for students to understand what entrepreneurship entails. At its core, entrepreneurship involves identifying opportunities, taking calculated risks, and creating value through the development of new products, services, or ventures. By grasping this definition, students can appreciate the diverse aspects of entrepreneurship beyond just starting a business.

Fostering an Entrepreneurial Mindset:

Entrepreneurship is more than just a career path; it's a mindset characterized by creativity, resilience, and adaptability. By cultivating an entrepreneurial mindset, students learn to approach challenges as opportunities, embrace failure as a learning experience, and continuously seek innovative solutions to problems. This mindset is invaluable not only in business but also in all aspects of life.

Exploring Entrepreneurial Traits and Characteristics:

Students should familiarize themselves with the traits and characteristics commonly associated with successful entrepreneurs. These may include traits such as passion, perseverance, self-discipline, and a willingness to take risks. By recognizing these traits within themselves, students can assess their own entrepreneurial potential and identify areas for personal development.

Understanding the Importance of Innovation:

Innovation lies at the heart of entrepreneurship. Students need to understand that entrepreneurship is not solely about replicating existing ideas but about creating something new and valuable. By fostering a culture of innovation, students can uncover opportunities for disruptive change and drive progress in various industries and sectors.

Learning from Entrepreneurial Role Models:

Studying the stories of successful entrepreneurs can provide valuable insights and inspiration for students. By learning from the experiences of others, students can gain a deeper understanding of the entrepreneurial journey, including its challenges, triumphs, and lessons learned along the way. This exposure to role models can help students envision their own paths to success.

Embracing Entrepreneurial Education and Resources:

Many educational institutions offer programs, courses, and resources focused on entrepreneurship. By taking advantage of these opportunities, students can gain practical knowledge, skills, and support networks to help them succeed as entrepreneurs. Additionally, leveraging online resources, books, and mentorship programs can further enhance students' understanding of entrepreneurship.

Recognizing the Global Impact of Entrepreneurship:

Entrepreneurship transcends geographic boundaries and has the prospective to drive positive change on a global scale. Students should recognize the impact that entrepreneurship can have in addressing pressing social, environmental, and economic challenges around the world. By understanding the global dimension of entrepreneurship, students can aspire to become change makers and contribute to a more sustainable and inclusive future.

Benefits of entrepreneurship for students

Entrepreneurship offers a superfluity of benefits for students, transcending traditional academic boundaries and providing invaluable opportunities for personal and professional growth. Here's a closer look at the benefits of entrepreneurship for students:

Hands-on Learning Experience:

Entrepreneurship provides students with a real-world, hands-on learning experience that complements classroom education. By starting and running their own businesses, students gain practical insights into various aspects of business management, including marketing, finance, operations, and customer service. This experiential learning fosters a deeper understanding of business concepts and enhances retention compared to traditional textbook learning.

Development of Practical Skills:

Engaging in entrepreneurial activities helps students develop a wide range of practical skills that are highly valued in today's job market. These skills include critical thinking, problem-solving, decision-making, communication, leadership, and time management. By navigating the challenges of entrepreneurship, students build resilience, adaptability, and resourcefulness, which are essential for success in any field.

Creativity and Innovation:

Entrepreneurship encourages students to think creatively, challenge the status quo, and innovate. By exploring business opportunities, students learn to identify unmet needs, envision new products or services, and develop innovative solutions to address them. This creativity and innovation drive progress, fuel economic growth, and contribute to societal advancement.

Empowerment and Self-Discovery:

Entrepreneurship empowers students to take control of their futures, pursue their passions, and realize their full potential. By starting and running their own businesses, students gain a sense of autonomy, self-confidence, and empowerment. Moreover, entrepreneurship offers a platform for self-discovery, allowing students to uncover their strengths, interests, and values as they navigate the entrepreneurial journey.

Financial Independence:

Entrepreneurship provides students with the opportunity to create their own sources of income and achieve financial independence. Rather than relying solely on part-time jobs or financial assistance, entrepreneurship enables students to generate revenue through their ventures. This financial autonomy not only alleviates financial pressures but also instills a sense of responsibility and fiscal discipline.

Networking and Relationship Building:

Entrepreneurship opens doors to valuable networking opportunities and allows students to connect with like-minded individuals, mentors, investors, and potential collaborators. Building a strong network of contacts not only facilitates the growth of their businesses but also lays the groundwork for future career opportunities and personal growth. Networking within the entrepreneurial community also exposes students to diverse perspectives and fosters a culture of collaboration and mutual support.

Creating Impact:

Entrepreneurship provides students with a platform to create meaningful impact in their communities and beyond. Whether by solving pressing social or environmental issues, supporting local economies, or inspiring others through their ventures, student entrepreneurs have the opportunity to make a positive difference in the world. By aligning their businesses with their values and passions, students can create ventures that not only generate profits but also generate positive social or environmental outcomes.

Myths and misconceptions about entrepreneurship

Dispelling myths and misconceptions about entrepreneurship is essential for aspiring entrepreneurs to make informed decisions and navigate the entrepreneurial landscape effectively. Here are some common myths and misconceptions about entrepreneurship:

Myth: Entrepreneurship is only for the wealthy or privileged.

Reality: While access to capital can be advantageous, entrepreneurship is not limited to those with significant financial resources. Many successful entrepreneurs have started with limited funds and built their businesses through creativity, resourcefulness, and determination. Additionally, various funding options, such as bootstrapping, crowdfunding, and grants, are available to aspiring entrepreneurs.

Myth: Entrepreneurship guarantees overnight success and wealth.

Reality: Entrepreneurship is often glamorized in the media, portraying overnight success stories and instant wealth. However, the reality is that building a successful business takes time, effort, and perseverance. Most successful entrepreneurs experience setbacks, failures, and years of hard work before achieving significant success. Patience, resilience, and a long-term perspective are essential qualities for aspiring entrepreneurs.

Myth: You need to have a groundbreaking idea to start a business.

Reality: While innovative ideas can certainly drive business success, not every successful business is based on a groundbreaking idea. Many successful entrepreneurs identify existing problems or needs in the market and develop solutions or improvements to address them. Additionally, execution and implementation are often more critical than the originality of the idea. Successful businesses are built on value creation, customer satisfaction, and effective execution.

Myth: Entrepreneurship is a solitary journey.

Reality: Entrepreneurship is often portrayed as a solitary pursuit, with the entrepreneur as the lone visionary leading the charge. In reality, successful entrepreneurs rely on a network of supporters, collaborators, mentors, and advisors to navigate challenges and capitalize on opportunities. Building a strong support network and collaborating with others are essential for entrepreneurial success.

Myth: Entrepreneurs are born, not made.

Reality: While some individuals may have inherent entrepreneurial traits or tendencies, entrepreneurship can be learned and cultivated through education, experience, and practice. Entrepreneurial skills, such as creativity, problem-solving, and leadership, can be developed over time through deliberate effort and continuous learning. Anyone with passion, determination, and a willingness to learn can become a successful entrepreneur.

Myth: Entrepreneurs must take big risks to succeed.

Reality: While entrepreneurship inherently involves risk-taking, successful entrepreneurs are tactical in managing and mitigating risks. Entrepreneurship is not about blindly taking big risks but rather about identifying and evaluating opportunities, assessing risks, and making informed decisions. Successful entrepreneurs take calculated risks, based on thorough research, analysis, and planning, to increase their chances of success.

Myth: Entrepreneurship is only for young people or tech-savvy individuals.

Reality: Entrepreneurship is not limited by age, background, or technical expertise. People of all ages and backgrounds can pursue entrepreneurship, and success can be achieved in various industries and sectors. While technology and innovation play a significant role in many entrepreneurial ventures, there are countless opportunities for non-tech-savvy individuals to start and grow successful businesses.

Chapter 3: Identifying Your Passion and Skills

Before diving into the world of entrepreneurship, it's essential to gain clarity on your interests, passions, and skills. This self-assessment process will serve as a foundation for identifying business opportunities that align with your strengths and aspirations.

1. Interest Inventory:

Begin by reflecting on the activities, subjects, or topics that genuinely captivate your attention. Ask yourself:

What hobbies or activities do I enjoy in my free time?

Which subjects do I find myself researching or reading about out of curiosity?

Are there any problems in my community or society that I feel passionate about solving?

Make a list of your interests, no matter how diverse they may seem. This inventory will help you uncover potential business ideas that resonate with your passions.

2. Passion Exploration:

Passion is the fuel that drives successful entrepreneurs. To identify your passions, consider the following exercises:

Recall moments in your life when you felt the most fulfilled or energized. What were you doing?

Think about causes or issues that evoke strong emotions in you. Why do they matter to you?

Imagine having unlimited resources and time. How would you choose to spend your days?

By delving into your deepest passions, you'll unearth opportunities to create businesses that are not only financially rewarding but also personally meaningful.

3. Skills Assessment:

Next, assess your strengths and competencies to determine how they can be leveraged in entrepreneurship:

What skills have I developed through my education, work experience, or personal projects?

What tasks or activities do others often seek my help with?

In which areas do I excel compared to my peers?

Discover both hard skills (technical abilities) and soft skills (communication, leadership) that set you apart. Recognizing your skill set will guide you in selecting business ventures that align with your expertise.

4. Values Clarification:

Consider your core values and beliefs as you explore potential business opportunities:

What principles do I hold dear in both my personal and professional life?

Are there causes or ethical considerations that I prioritize when making decisions?

How do I envision my business contributing to the greater good or making a positive impact?

Aligning your business endeavors with your values ensures a sense of fulfillment and purpose beyond financial success.

5. Feedback Gathering:

Lastly, seek input from trusted friends, mentors, or colleagues who know you well. Ask for their perspectives on your interests, passions, and skills. Their insights may provide valuable clarity and perspective as you navigate your entrepreneurial journey.

Understanding how personal interests can drive business opportunities

Understanding how personal interests can drive business opportunities is a fundamental aspect of entrepreneurial success. When you build a business around something you're genuinely passionate about, your enthusiasm becomes a powerful catalyst for innovation, resilience, and long-term commitment. In this chapter, we explore how to identify and leverage your personal interests to uncover lucrative business ventures.

1. Identifying Personal Passions:

The first step in harnessing personal interests for business is to identify what truly excites and motivates you. Reflect on activities, hobbies, or subjects that ignite your curiosity and enthusiasm. Whether it's a love for technology, a passion for cooking, or a deep-rooted interest in sustainability, your personal passions hold valuable clues to potential business opportunities.

2. Aligning Passion with Market Demand:

While personal passions provide the spark for entrepreneurship, it's essential to ensure alignment with market demand. Conduct thorough market research to identify areas where your interests intersect with consumer needs and preferences. Look for niche markets or underserved demographics that can benefit from your unique perspective and expertise.

3. Leveraging Expertise and Knowledge:

Your personal interests often coincide with areas where you have acquired expertise or specialized knowledge. Whether through formal education, professional experience, or self-directed learning, your skills and insights can serve as valuable assets in entrepreneurship. Leverage your expertise to develop innovative solutions, create compelling products or services, and differentiate yourself in the market.

4. Solving Personal Pain Points:

Entrepreneurship is often born out of a desire to solve personal pain points or address challenges faced in your own life. Consider the problems or frustrations you encounter on a daily basis and explore opportunities to develop solutions that not only benefit you but also have broader market potential. By addressing genuine needs and offering meaningful solutions, you can create businesses that resonate with customers on a personal level.

5. Fostering Authenticity and Connection:

Building a business around your personal interests allows you to authentically connect with your audience and build a loyal customer base. Authenticity breeds trust and credibility, fostering deeper connections with customers who share your passions and values. Embrace your unique voice, story, and perspective to create authentic brand experiences that resonate with your target market.

6. Cultivating Passion-Driven Innovation:

Passion-driven entrepreneurship fuels advancement and creativity, driving continuous improvement and adaptation. When you're deeply invested in your business's mission and purpose, you're more likely to embrace challenges as opportunities for growth and innovation. Cultivate a culture of curiosity, experimentation, and passion-driven innovation to stay ahead of the curve and maintain a competitive edge.

7. Embracing Evolution and Exploration:

As your interests and passions evolve over time, so too may your business opportunities. Embrace change and remain open to new possibilities, continually exploring different avenues for growth and expansion. Stay connected with your audience, solicit feedback, and adapt your business strategies to align with shifting market dynamics and emerging trends.

Leveraging existing skills and knowledge

One of the greatest assets you bring to entrepreneurship is your existing skills and knowledge. Whether gained through formal education, work experience, or personal endeavors, these competencies provide a solid foundation for identifying and seizing business opportunities. In this chapter, we explore how to leverage your existing skills and knowledge to propel your entrepreneurial journey forward.

1. Assessing Your Skill Set:

Begin by conducting a comprehensive assessment of your skills, both technical and soft. Consider your strengths, areas of expertise, and any specialized knowledge you possess. This self-awareness is crucial for identifying areas where you can add value and excel as an entrepreneur.

2. Identifying Transferable Skills:

While some skills may be directly applicable to your chosen business venture, others may be transferable across different industries or domains. For example, project management, communication, and problem-solving skills are highly transferable and can be leveraged in various entrepreneurial endeavors. Identify the transferable skills you possess and explore how they can be applied in the context of your business.

3. Capitalizing on Specialized Knowledge:

Specialized knowledge acquired through education, training, or work experience can give you a competitive edge in your chosen niche. Whether it's expertise in a particular field, proficiency with specific technologies, or insights gained from industry experience, capitalize on your specialized knowledge to differentiate yourself in the market and position yourself as an authority in your field.

4. Expanding Your Skill Set:

Entrepreneurship is a journey of continuous learning and growth. Identify areas where you can further develop your skills to enhance your entrepreneurial capabilities. This may involve pursuing additional training, attending workshops or seminars, or seeking mentorship from experienced professionals. By expanding your skill set, you not only increase your value as an entrepreneur but also position yourself for long-term success.

5. Leveraging Networks and Resources:

Your existing networks and resources can also play a crucial role in your entrepreneurial endeavors. Tap into your professional network, alumni connections, and industry associations to access valuable resources, mentorship opportunities, and potential collaborators. Leverage these networks to gain insights, gather feedback, and forge strategic partnerships that can accelerate your business growth.

6. Embracing a Growth Mindset:

Entrepreneurship requires a growth mindset—an attitude of continuous improvement, resilience, and adaptability. Embrace challenges as opportunities for learning and growth, and be willing to step outside your comfort zone to acquire new skills and knowledge. Cultivate a mindset of curiosity, creativity, and perseverance as you navigate the ups and downs of entrepreneurship.

7. Celebrating Your Unique Value Proposition:

Your unique combination of skills, knowledge, and experiences forms the foundation of your value proposition as an entrepreneur. Celebrate what sets you apart from others and leverage it as a competitive advantage. Whether it's your technical expertise, industry insights, or creative talents, communicate your unique value proposition effectively to attract customers, investors, and collaborators.

Chapter4: . Exploring Different Business Models

As a student entrepreneur, choosing the right business model is crucial for launching and sustaining your venture amidst academic responsibilities and limited resources. In this chapter, we provide an overview of various business models tailored to the unique needs and constraints of students.

1. Freelancing and Service-Based Businesses:

Freelancing offers students a flexible way to monetize their skills and expertise on a project-by-project basis. Whether it's graphic design, writing, programming, or tutoring, students can offer their services to clients locally or online. Service-based businesses allow students to leverage their existing skills and knowledge while setting their own schedules to accommodate academic commitments.

2. E-Commerce and Dropshipping:

E-commerce platforms provide students with opportunities to sell products online without the need for inventory or upfront capital. Dropshipping, in particular, allows students to partner with suppliers to fulfill orders directly to customers, eliminating the need for warehousing and shipping logistics. With the rise of online marketplaces and social media marketing, students can easily launch and scale e-commerce ventures from their dorm rooms.

3. Subscription-Based Models:

Subscription-based businesses offer a recurring revenue stream by providing customers with access to products or services on a subscription basis. Students can create subscription boxes, digital content platforms, or membership communities tailored to niche interests or hobbies. Subscription models provide predictable revenue and foster long-term customer relationships, making them ideal for student entrepreneurs seeking sustainable growth.

4. Online Courses and Digital Products:

Students can capitalize on their expertise and knowledge by creating and selling online courses, e-books, or digital products. With platforms like Udemy, Teachable, and Gumroad, students can easily create and market educational content to a global audience. Digital products require minimal overhead and can generate passive income, making them an attractive option for students looking to monetize their skills and expertise.

5. Social Impact Ventures:

Social impact ventures allow students to pursue entrepreneurial endeavors while making a positive difference in their communities or the world. Whether it's launching a nonprofit organization, a social enterprise, or a sustainable business, students can combine their passion for social change with innovative business models. Social impact ventures attract socially conscious consumers and investors, providing students with opportunities to create meaningful impact while building successful businesses.

6. Collaborative and Sharing Economy Platforms:

Students can leverage collaborative and sharing economy platforms to create businesses that facilitate resource sharing, peer-to-peer transactions, or collaborative consumption. Whether it's ride-sharing, accommodation rentals, or peer-to-peer tutoring, collaborative platforms enable students to monetize underutilized assets or skills while fostering community engagement and trust.

7. Hybrid Models and Innovations:

Innovation knows no bounds, and students are uniquely positioned to experiment with hybrid business models and disruptive innovations. Whether it's combining elements of different business models, leveraging emerging technologies, or addressing unmet needs in untapped markets, students can create innovative ventures that defy traditional business paradigms.

Examples of Successful Student Entrepreneurs

While balancing academics and entrepreneurship can be challenging, many students have successfully navigated this dual journey to build thriving businesses. In this chapter, we showcase inspiring examples of student entrepreneurs who turned their innovative ideas into successful ventures, demonstrating the potential for entrepreneurial success at a young age.

1. Mark Zuckerberg - Facebook:

Perhaps one of the most famous examples of student entrepreneurship is Mark Zuckerberg, who co-founded Facebook while studying at Harvard University. What started as a social networking platform for college students in 2004 quickly grew into a global phenomenon, revolutionizing the way people connect and communicate online. Zuckerberg's vision and relentless pursuit of innovation propelled Facebook to become one of the most influential companies in the world.

2. Michael Dell - Dell Technologies:

Michael Dell founded Dell Technologies from his dorm room at the University of Texas at Austin in 1984. Recognizing the potential of direct-to-consumer sales and customization in the computer industry, Dell pioneered the concept of selling PCs directly to customers, bypassing traditional retail channels. His entrepreneurial spirit and commitment to customer-centric innovation transformed Dell into a leading global technology company.

3. Evan Spiegel, Bobby Murphy, and Reggie Brown - Snapchat:

Evan Spiegel, Bobby Murphy, and Reggie Brown launched Snapchat while studying at Stanford University in 2011. The photo-sharing app, known for its disappearing messages and innovative features, quickly gained popularity among young users worldwide. Despite facing initial skepticism, Spiegel and his co-founders persevered, leveraging their insights into millennial behavior to build a multibillion-dollar social media platform.

4. Ben Silbermann - Pinterest:

Ben Silbermann co-founded Pinterest while attending Yale University in 2009. Inspired by his love for collecting and organizing visual inspiration, Silbermann envisioned a platform where users could discover and share ideas through curated collections of images. With a focus on simplicity and visual discovery, Pinterest grew into a beloved social media platform with millions of users worldwide, showcasing the power of passion-driven entrepreneurship.

5. Brian Chesky, Joe Gebbia, and Nathan Blecharczyk - Airbnb:

Brian Chesky, Joe Gebbia, and Nathan Blecharczyk launched Airbnb while attending the Rhode Island School of Design and the Harvard Graduate School of Design. Faced with the challenge of affording rent in expensive cities, the trio came up with the idea of renting out air mattresses in their apartment to travelers. This concept evolved into Airbnb, a peer-to-peer lodging marketplace that has transformed the way people travel and experience new destinations.

6. Catherine Cook - MyYearbook (Now MeetMe):

Catherine Cook co-founded MyYearbook, a social networking site for teenagers, while she was still in high school. Recognizing the need for a platform where young people could connect and share experiences, Cook and her brother launched MyYearbook in 2005. The platform gained rapid traction among teenagers, eventually evolving into MeetMe, a leading social discovery app with millions of users worldwide.

7. Palmer Luckey - Oculus VR:

Palmer Luckey, a college dropout and self-taught engineer, founded Oculus VR in 2012. Inspired by his passion for virtual reality technology, Luckey developed the Oculus Rift, a groundbreaking virtual reality headset that revolutionized the gaming and entertainment industries. Oculus VR was later acquired by Facebook for $2 billion, cementing Luckey's place as a pioneer in the field of virtual reality.

Chapter 5: Researching Market Opportunities

Researching market opportunities is a critical step in the entrepreneurial journey, allowing students to identify viable business ideas and validate their potential for success. In this chapter, we delve into the process of market research and provide actionable strategies for students to uncover promising market opportunities.

1. Understanding Market Dynamics:

Before diving into market research, it's essential to gain a solid understanding of the broader market dynamics relevant to your business idea. Consider factors such as industry trends, consumer behavior, competitive landscape, and regulatory environment. By analyzing market dynamics, students can identify emerging opportunities and potential challenges that may impact their ventures.

2. Defining Target Markets:

Define your target market—the specific group of customers or users who are most likely to benefit from your product or service. Conduct demographic, psychographic, and behavioral research to profile your target audience and gain insights into their needs, preferences, and pain points. Understanding your target market allows you to tailor your offerings and marketing strategies to effectively address their needs and capture their attention.

3. Conducting Primary Research:

Primary research involves gathering firsthand data directly from potential customers, industry experts, and other relevant stakeholders. Methods of primary research include surveys, interviews, focus groups, and observation. Engage with your target audience to collect valuable feedback, validate assumptions, and uncover insights that can inform product development, pricing strategies, and market positioning.

4. Analyzing Secondary Sources:

Secondary research involves gathering existing data from sources such as market reports, industry publications, academic journals, and government databases. Analyze secondary sources to gain insights into market trends, competitor analysis, consumer behavior, and macroeconomic factors. By leveraging existing data, students can supplement their primary research efforts and gain a comprehensive understanding of the market landscape.

5. Identifying Unmet Needs and Gaps:

Look for unmet needs, underserved niches, or gaps in the market where existing solutions fall short. Conduct competitive analysis to assess the strengths and weaknesses of competing offerings and identify areas where you can differentiate your product or service. By addressing unmet needs and offering unique value propositions, students can carve out their own space in the market and attract customers seeking innovative solutions.

6. Evaluating Market Viability:

Assess the viability of potential market opportunities based on factors such as market size, growth potential, competitive intensity, and barriers to entry. Use tools such as SWOT analysis (Strengths, Weaknesses, Opportunities, Threats) and Porter's Five Forces framework to evaluate the attractiveness of market segments and identify strategic opportunities. By evaluating market viability, students can make informed decisions about which opportunities to pursue and allocate resources effectively.

7. Iterating and Refining:

Market research is an iterative process that requires continuous learning and refinement. Be open to feedback, adapt to changing market conditions, and iterate on your business ideas based on new insights and data. Embrace a mindset of experimentation and agility, and be willing to pivot or adjust your strategies as needed to seize emerging opportunities and mitigate risks.

Conducting market research as a student entrepreneur

As a student entrepreneur, conducting effective market research is crucial for identifying viable business opportunities, understanding customer needs, and positioning your venture for success. In this chapter, we explore practical strategies and tips for conducting market research tailored to the unique constraints and opportunities faced by student entrepreneurs.

1. Define Your Research Objectives:

Before diving into market research, clearly define your research objectives and questions. What are you trying to learn or validate? Are you exploring potential market demand for a new product or service? Are you assessing customer preferences or pricing sensitivity? Establishing clear research objectives will guide your efforts and ensure that you gather relevant insights to inform your business decisions.

2. Leverage University Resources:

Take advantage of the resources available to you as a student, including university libraries, databases, and research centers. Access academic journals, industry reports, and market analysis tools to gather secondary data and gain insights into market trends, competitor analysis, and consumer behavior. University faculty and mentors can also provide valuable guidance and support for your research efforts.

3. Tap into Student Networks:

Harness the power of your student network to gather firsthand insights from your peers and potential customers. Conduct surveys, interviews, or focus groups to collect feedback on your business idea, product concepts, or marketing messaging. Engage with student organizations, clubs, and campus events to connect with diverse perspectives and gather valuable input for your market research.

4. Utilize Online Tools and Platforms:

Explore online tools and platforms to conduct market research efficiently and cost-effectively. Use survey tools like SurveyMonkey or Google Forms to collect quantitative data from a large audience. Leverage social media platforms, online forums, and student groups to gather qualitative insights, engage with potential customers, and observe online conversations related to your industry or niche.

5. Test Minimum Viable Products (MVPs):

Develop minimum viable products (MVPs) or prototypes to test your business idea and gather real-world feedback from customers. Create landing pages, mockups, or prototypes to showcase your product or service and gauge interest and demand. Use techniques like A/B testing or beta launches to iterate on your offerings based on customer feedback and refine your value proposition.

6. Conduct Competitor Analysis:

Analyze competitors operating in your target market to understand their strengths, weaknesses, and market positioning. Identify direct and indirect competitors, assess their product offerings, pricing strategies, and customer engagement tactics. By conducting competitive analysis, you can identify opportunities for differentiation, uncover market gaps, and refine your business strategy to gain a competitive edge.

7. Stay Agile and Iterate:

Market research is an ongoing process that requires quickness, adaptability, and continuous learning. Stay open to feedback, iterate on your research methods, and adjust your strategies based on new insights and data. Be willing to pivot or refine your business idea as you gather more information and gain a deeper understanding of market dynamics and customer needs.

Identifying niche markets and trends

Identifying niche markets and emerging trends is a strategic approach for student entrepreneurs to uncover lucrative business opportunities with less competition and greater potential for growth. In this chapter, we explore techniques and strategies for identifying niche markets and staying abreast of emerging trends in various industries.

1. Conduct Market Segmentation:

Begin by segmenting broader markets into smaller, more specialized segments or niches. Look for underserved or overlooked customer segments with specific needs, preferences, or pain points that are not adequately addressed by existing solutions. By identifying niche markets within larger industries, student entrepreneurs can tailor their offerings to meet the unique needs of these niche audiences.

2. Leverage Personal Experience and Passion:

Draw upon your personal experiences, interests, and passions to identify niche markets that resonate with you. Reflect on hobbies, interests, or problems you've encountered in your own life, and explore opportunities to create solutions that cater to niche audiences with similar interests or challenges. By aligning your business with your personal passions, you're more likely to stay motivated and connected to your target market.

3. Monitor Industry Trends and Insights:

Stay informed about industry trends, market dynamics, and consumer behavior by monitoring industry publications, market research reports, and relevant online forums and communities. Subscribe to newsletters, follow industry influencers, and participate in industry events to stay abreast of emerging trends and developments. By staying ahead of the curve, student entrepreneurs can capitalize on emerging opportunities before they become mainstream.

4. Analyze Data and Metrics:

Utilize data analysis tools and metrics to identify patterns, trends, and opportunities within your target market. Analyze data from social media platforms, website analytics, and market research surveys to uncover insights into consumer behavior, preferences, and purchasing patterns. By leveraging data-driven insights, student entrepreneurs can make informed decisions and tailor their strategies to capitalize on emerging trends.

5. Explore Cross-Industry Insights:

Look beyond your immediate industry or niche to identify cross-industry insights and trends that may present opportunities for innovation and diversification. Explore how trends in technology, consumer behavior, or societal shifts may impact various industries and create opportunities for new products, services, or business models. By connecting the dots between different industries, student entrepreneurs can uncover unique perspectives and innovative ideas.

6. Seek Feedback and Validation:

Engage with potential customers, industry experts, and mentors to gather feedback and validate your ideas and assumptions. Conduct surveys, interviews, or focus groups to solicit input from your target market and assess demand for your offerings. Seek feedback from experienced entrepreneurs, industry professionals, and academic advisors to gain valuable insights and perspectives on market trends and opportunities.

7. Stay Flexible and Adaptive:

Remain flexible and adaptive in your approach to identifying niche markets and emerging trends. Markets are constantly evolving, and what may be a niche opportunity today could become main stream tomorrow. Stay open to new ideas, pivot when necessary, and be willing to experiment and iterate as you navigate the dynamic landscape of entrepreneurship.

Tools and resources for market analysis

Market analysis is a crucial component of entrepreneurial success, providing valuable insights into industry trends, customer preferences, and competitive landscapes. In this chapter, we explore a variety of tools and resources that student entrepreneurs can leverage to conduct comprehensive market analysis and make informed business decisions.

1. Market Research Platforms:

Market research platforms such as IBISWorld, Statista, and MarketResearch.com provide access to comprehensive industry reports, market data, and trend analysis across various sectors. These platforms offer valuable insights into market size, growth projections, competitive dynamics, and key success factors, allowing student entrepreneurs to conduct in-depth market research and identify opportunities for growth and innovation.

2. Survey and Polling Tools:

Survey and polling tools like SurveyMonkey, Google Forms, and Typeform enable student entrepreneurs to collect quantitative data from target audiences and gather insights into consumer preferences, purchasing behavior, and product feedback. These tools allow for the creation of customizable surveys and questionnaires, as well as data analysis features to interpret survey results and identify trends.

3. Social Media Listening Tools:

Social media listening tools such as Hootsuite, Brandwatch, and Mention provide student entrepreneurs with the ability to monitor online conversations, sentiment, and trends related to their industry, brand, or competitors. These tools track mentions, hashtags, and keywords across social media platforms, allowing entrepreneurs to gather real-time insights, engage with customers, and identify emerging trends and opportunities.

4. Google Trends:

Google Trends is a free tool that allows student entrepreneurs to explore search trends and patterns across different regions and time periods. By analyzing search volume data for specific keywords or topics, entrepreneurs can identify rising trends, seasonal fluctuations, and geographic variations in consumer interest. Google Trends also provides related queries and topics, offering additional insights into consumer behavior and interests.

5. Industry Associations and Reports:

Industry associations and trade publications often publish industry reports, whitepapers, and research studies that provide valuable insights into market trends, regulatory developments, and best practices within specific sectors. Student entrepreneurs can leverage these resources to stay informed about industry dynamics, network with industry professionals, and access specialized knowledge and expertise.

6. Academic Research Databases:

Academic research databases such as JSTOR, ProQuest, and PubMed offer access to scholarly articles, journals, and research papers across a wide range of disciplines. These databases provide student entrepreneurs with access to cutting-edge research, theoretical frameworks, and empirical studies relevant to their industry or business idea. By exploring academic literature, entrepreneurs can gain a deeper understanding of market dynamics and consumer behavior.

7. Online Courses and Tutorials:

Online courses and tutorials on platforms like Coursera, Udemy, and LinkedIn Learning offer valuable resources for student entrepreneurs looking to enhance their market analysis skills. These courses cover topics such as market research methodologies, data analysis techniques, and industry-specific insights, providing practical knowledge and tools to conduct effective market analysis and make data-driven decisions.

8. Entrepreneurial Communities and Networks:

Entrepreneurial communities, forums, and networking groups provide student entrepreneurs with opportunities to connect with like-minded individuals, share insights and experiences, and access valuable resources and support. Platforms like Reddit, Quora, and startup incubators offer forums for asking questions, seeking advice, and collaborating with other entrepreneurs, mentors, and industry experts.

Chapter 6: Developing Business Ideas

In the journey of entrepreneurship, one of the crucial steps is refining business ideas to ensure they align with personal interests, skills, and market opportunities. This process not only enhances the chances of success but also fosters passion and commitment towards the venture. Let's delve into the essential considerations and strategies for refining business ideas effectively.

Identifying Personal Interests:

Start by introspecting and identifying your passions, hobbies, and interests. What activities excite you? What topics do you find yourself constantly exploring or discussing?

Consider your past experiences and the activities that bring you joy. Whether it's cooking, technology, fashion, or environmental sustainability, your genuine interest will drive motivation and creativity in your business endeavor.

Assessing Skills and Expertise:

Take inventory of your skills, knowledge, and expertise. What are you naturally good at? What skills have you acquired through education, work, or personal development?

Assess how your skills can be leveraged in a business context. For instance, if you have a knack for graphic design, you could explore opportunities in freelance design services or creating digital products.

Researching Market Opportunities:

Conduct thorough market research to identify potential opportunities and gaps in the industry related to your interests and skills.

Analyze consumer needs, preferences, and trends within your target market. Look for areas where your unique perspective or offering can fulfill unmet demands or improve existing solutions.

Aligning Interests with Market Demand:

Evaluate the feasibility and viability of your business ideas by considering their alignment with market demand. Are there enough potential customers interested in your product or service?

Look for ways to tailor your interests and skills to meet market needs effectively. This might involve refining your business model, adjusting your offerings, or targeting niche market segments.

Seeking Feedback and Validation:

Share your business ideas with trusted mentors, peers, or potential customers to gather feedback and validation. Listen attentively to their perspectives and insights.

Use opinion to iterate and refine your business concept further. Pay attention to recurring themes or suggestions that can help strengthen your idea and increase its appeal in the market.

Testing and Iterating:

Consider prototyping or conducting small-scale tests to validate your business idea before fully committing resources. This could involve creating a minimum viable product (MVP) or offering pilot services to gauge customer interest and feedback.

Be open to iterating and adapting your business idea based on real-world feedback and data. Flexibility and agility are essential traits in refining and optimizing your venture for success.

Creating a unique value proposition

In the crowded marketplace of today, where countless businesses vie for consumer attention, creating a unique value proposition is essential for standing out from the competition and capturing the hearts and minds of your target audience. A well-crafted value proposition succinctly communicates the distinctive benefits and value your product or service offers to customers. Let's explore the key components and strategies for creating a compelling value proposition.

Understanding Customer Needs and Pain Points:

Start by gaining a deep understanding of your target customers' needs, desires, and pain points. What challenges are they facing? What are they looking for in a solution?

Conduct market research, surveys, and interviews to gather insights into customer preferences, behaviors, and motivations. Use this information to inform the development of your value proposition.

Identifying Points of Differentiation:

Analyze your product or service offerings and identify what sets them apart from competitors. This could include unique features, superior quality, innovative technology, exceptional customer service, or a distinctive brand identity.

Highlight your competitive advantages and points of differentiation that address specific customer needs or pain points more effectively than alternatives in the market.

Articulating Clear and Concise Benefits:

Craft a value proposition that clearly communicates the benefits and outcomes customers can expect from choosing your offering. Focus on how your product or service solves their problems, fulfills their desires, or improves their lives.

Use simple, jargon-free language that resonates with your target audience and clearly articulates the value proposition's relevance and significance to them.

Emphasizing Unique Selling Proposition (USP):

Define your unique selling proposition (USP), which encapsulates the single most compelling reason why customers should choose your offering over alternatives. This could be based on a specific feature, benefit, or brand attribute that resonates strongly with your target market.

Communicate your USP prominently in your value proposition to grab attention and differentiate your brand from competitors in the minds of consumers.

Addressing Emotional and Rational Drivers:

Appeal to both emotional and rational drivers in your value proposition. While rational benefits such as cost savings or efficiency are important, emotional appeals such as convenience, status, or peace of mind can also play a significant role in influencing purchasing decisions.

Understand the emotional triggers and aspirations of your target audience and incorporate them into your value proposition to create a deeper connection and resonance with customers.

Testing and Iterating:

Continuously test and refine your value proposition based on feedback from customers, market trends, and competitive analysis. Monitor how effectively your value proposition resonates with your target audience and adjust as needed to optimize its effectiveness.

Be willing to iterate and evolve your value proposition over time to stay relevant and competitive in a dynamic market landscape.

Prototyping and testing your business concept

Prototyping and testing your business concept is a critical phase in the entrepreneurial journey, serving as a bridge between ideation and execution. This iterative process allows you to gather valuable feedback, validate assumptions, and refine your idea before investing significant resources. Let's explore the steps involved in prototyping and testing your business concept effectively.

Define Your Hypotheses:

Start by clearly defining the key assumptions and hypotheses underlying your business concept. These could include assumptions about customer needs, market demand, competitive landscape, pricing strategy, and distribution channels.

Identify the most critical hypotheses that need to be validated to mitigate risks and increase the likelihood of success.

Create a Prototype:

Develop a prototype or minimum viable product (MVP) that allows you to test your business concept in a real-world context with minimal resources. The goal is to create a simplified version of your product or service that demonstrates its core functionality and value proposition.

Depending on your business idea, your prototype could range from a physical product prototype to a mockup of a website or mobile app.

Select Testing Methods:

Choose appropriate methods for testing your prototype and validating your hypotheses. This could involve conducting user interviews, surveys, focus groups, usability testing, A/B testing, or launching a pilot program.

Select methods that align with your target audience, the nature of your business concept, and the insights you aim to gather.

Engage with Potential Customers:

Engage directly with potential customers to gather feedback on your prototype. This could involve reaching out to your target audience through various channels, such as social media, community events, or industry forums.

Encourage open and honest feedback from users about their experience with your prototype, including likes, dislikes, pain points, and suggestions for improvement.

Iterate Based on Feedback:

Analyze the feedback collected from testing and identify patterns, insights, and areas for improvement. Pay close attention to both positive feedback and constructive criticism.

Use feedback to iterate and refine your prototype, making adjustments to address identified issues, enhance user experience, and better align with customer needs and preferences.

Measure Key Metrics:

Define key metrics and performance indicators to track during the testing phase. These metrics could include customer engagement, conversion rates, user satisfaction, retention rates, and revenue generation.

Continuously monitor and analyze these metrics to assess the effectiveness of your prototype and identify opportunities for optimization.

Iterate and Test Again:

Iterate through multiple rounds of prototyping and testing, incorporating feedback and insights gained from each iteration. The goal is to refine your business idea iteratively until you achieve product-market fit and validation of your key hypotheses.

Be prepared to pivot or make significant adjustments to your concept based on the learning and discoveries made during the testing process.

Chapter 7: Building a Business Plan

For student entrepreneurs, embarking on the journey of starting a business requires careful planning and strategic thinking. A well-crafted business plan serves as a roadmap to guide your venture from ideation to execution, helping you clarify your vision, set goals, and secure resources. Here are the essential components of a business plan tailored specifically for student entrepreneurs:

Executive Summary:

Provide a concise overview of your business concept, including the problem you're solving, your solution, target market, competitive advantage, and objectives.

Summarize key highlights of your business plan, such as financial projections, marketing strategies, and milestones.

Business Description:

Describe your business idea in detail, including the products or services you'll offer, your target market, unique selling proposition, and the value you'll deliver to customers.

Explain the inspiration behind your business idea and how it aligns with your passions, skills, and academic pursuits.

Market Analysis:

Conduct thorough market research to analyze industry trends, customer demographics, market size, competition, and potential growth opportunities.

Identify your target market segments and their needs, preferences, and purchasing behaviors. Assess the demand for your products or services and potential barriers to entry.

Competitive Analysis:

Identify and analyze direct and indirect competitors in your industry. Evaluate their strengths, weaknesses, market positioning, pricing strategies, and customer feedback.

Highlight your competitive advantages and how you'll differentiate your business from competitors to capture market share.

Marketing and Sales Strategy:

Outline your marketing and sales strategies for acquiring customers and generating revenue. Define your target audience, channels, messaging, and promotional tactics.

Develop a comprehensive marketing plan that includes online and offline strategies, social media engagement, content marketing, advertising, and partnerships.

Operations Plan:

Detail the operational aspects of your business, including your organizational structure, key team members, roles, responsibilities, and workflow.

Describe your production processes, supply chain management, technology infrastructure, and any facilities or equipment required to operate your business.

Financial Projections:

Prepare financial forecasts for your business, including income statements, cash flow projections, and balance sheets. Estimate startup costs, operating expenses, sales projections, and profitability.

Include a break-even analysis and sensitivity analysis to assess the financial viability of your business under different scenarios.

Risk Management:

Identify potential risks and challenges that could impact your business's success, such as market volatility, regulatory changes, financial constraints, or operational disruptions.

Develop strategies to mitigate these risks and contingency plans to address unexpected challenges as they arise.

Timeline and Milestones:

Create a timeline outlining key milestones and objectives for launching and growing your business. Set measurable goals and deadlines to follow progress and hold yourself accountable.

Break down your timeline into short-term and long-term goals, such as product development milestones, marketing campaigns, revenue targets, and expansion plans.

Appendices:

Include any supplemental information or supporting documents relevant to your business plan, such as resumes of key team members, market research data, product prototypes, or legal documents.

Appendices provide additional context and credibility to your business plan, but keep them concise and relevant to the overall narrative.

Writing a mission statement and setting SMART goals

A mission statement encapsulates the core purpose, values, and aspirations of your business. It defines what your endeavor stands for and the impact it seeks to make in the world. Here's how to craft a meaningful mission statement:

Define Your Purpose: Reflect on the overarching reason why your business exists. What problem are you solving? What value are you delivering to customers or society?

Clarify Your Values: Identify the principles and beliefs that guide your actions and decision-making as an entrepreneur. What ethical standards do you uphold? What qualities do you want your brand to embody?

Articulate Your Vision: Envision the future state you aim to create through your business. What positive change do you aspire to achieve? How do you envision your business impacting the lives of your customers, employees, and community?

Be Concise and Memorable: Keep your mission statement succinct and memorable, using clear and compelling language that resonates with your target audience. Aim for clarity and authenticity to communicate your genuine intentions.

Inspire and Motivate: Craft a mission statement that inspires passion and commitment among stakeholders, including employees, customers, investors, and partners. It should rally people around a shared purpose and unite them in pursuit of a common goal.

Setting SMART Goals:

SMART goals are specific, measurable, achievable, relevant, and time-bound. They provide a framework for setting objectives that are clear, actionable, and attainable. Here's how to set SMART goals for your entrepreneurial endeavors:

Specific: Define your goals with clarity and precision. Clearly articulate what you want to accomplish and why it matters. Avoid vague or ambiguous language.

Measurable: Establish concrete criteria for measuring progress and success. Define metrics or key performance indicators (KPIs) that enable you to track your performance and determine whether you've achieved your goals.

Achievable: Set goals that are realistic and attainable given your resources, capabilities, and constraints. Consider the time, effort, and resources required to reach each goal, and ensure they are within your grasp.

Relevant: Align your goals with your mission, vision, and overarching strategic objectives. Ensure that each goal contributes meaningfully to your overall business strategy and priorities.

Time-Bound: Set deadlines or timeframes for achieving your goals. Establish clear timelines and milestones to keep yourself accountable and maintain a sense of urgency.

Example:

Mission Statement: "To empower individuals to lead healthier lives by providing access to nutritious and affordable meals, while fostering a sustainable food system that preserves our planet for future generations."

SMART Goal: "Increase customer engagement by 20% within six months by implementing a targeted digital marketing campaign, measured through website traffic, email open rates, and social media interactions."

Financial planning and budgeting

Financial planning and budgeting are vital components of entrepreneurial success, providing a roadmap for managing resources, maximizing profitability, and achieving long-term sustainability. Whether launching a startup or scaling an existing business, effective financial planning is essential for making informed decisions and navigating the complexities of the marketplace. Let's explore key strategies and best practices for financial planning and budgeting:

Establish Clear Financial Goals:

Define your financial objectives, both short-term and long-term. This could include revenue targets, profit margins, expense management goals, investment priorities, and growth projections.

Ensure that your financial goals are aligned with your overall business strategy and vision, guiding your decisions and resource allocation.

Create a Comprehensive Budget:

Develop a detailed budget that outlines your anticipated income and expenses across all aspects of your business operations. This includes costs related to production, marketing, sales, overhead, personnel, and capital expenditures.

Use historical data, market research, and industry benchmarks to estimate your expenses accurately. Factor in variable costs, such as materials or utilities, as well as fixed costs like rent or salaries.

Monitor Cash Flow:

Cash flow management is crucial for maintaining liquidity and sustaining day-to-day operations. Monitor your cash inflows and outflows regularly to ensure sufficient funds are available to cover expenses, repay debts, and invest in growth opportunities.

Identify potential cash flow bottlenecks or seasonal fluctuations and implement strategies to mitigate risks, such as securing lines of credit or negotiating payment terms with suppliers.

Allocate Resources Wisely:

Prioritize resource allocation based on your business priorities and financial goals. Allocate funds strategically to areas that contribute most to revenue generation, customer satisfaction, and long-term value creation.

Avoid overspending or unnecessary expenses by scrutinizing every expenditure and evaluating its potential return on investment (ROI) or impact on business performance.

Plan for Contingencies:

Anticipate unforeseen events or challenges that could impact your financial stability, such as economic downturns, market shifts, or regulatory changes. Develop contingency plans and set aside emergency funds to weather periods of uncertainty.

Consider obtaining business insurance coverage to protect against risks such as property damage, liability claims, or business interruption.

Review and Adjust Regularly:

Financial planning is an iterative process that requires ongoing review and adjustment. Regularly monitor your financial performance against budgeted targets and key performance indicators (KPIs).

Identify variances or deviations from your plan and take corrective actions as needed. This could involve cutting costs, optimizing pricing strategies, diversifying revenue streams, or reallocating resources to more profitable areas.

Invest in Financial Literacy:

Invest in developing your financial literacy and expertise as an entrepreneur. Familiarize yourself with basic accounting principles, financial ratios, and key financial metrics to make informed decisions and communicate effectively with stakeholders.

Consider seeking advice from financial professionals, such as accountants, financial advisors, or business mentors, to gain insights and perspectives on complex financial matters.

Chapter 8: Navigating Challenges and Overcoming Obstacles

Embarking on the entrepreneurial journey as a student comes with its own set of unique challenges and obstacles. While the experience offers immense opportunities for growth, innovation, and learning, it also requires resilience, resourcefulness, and adaptability to overcome the inevitable hurdles along the way. Let's explore some of the common challenges faced by student entrepreneurs and strategies for addressing them:

Time Management:

Balancing academic commitments, extracurricular activities, and entrepreneurial pursuits can be overwhelming for student entrepreneurs. Managing time effectively becomes crucial to juggle competing priorities and meet deadlines.

Strategies: Prioritize tasks, create a structured schedule, delegate responsibilities where possible, and leverage time management tools and techniques to optimize productivity and maintain a healthy work-life balance.

Limited Resources:

Students often have limited access to financial resources, industry connections, and professional networks compared to established entrepreneurs. Securing funding, attracting talent, and gaining traction in the marketplace can pose significant challenges.

Strategies: Explore alternative funding sources such as grants, crowdfunding, competitions, or student entrepreneurship programs. Build relationships with mentors, faculty members, alumni, and local entrepreneurship communities to access guidance, support, and opportunities.

Lack of Experience:

Student entrepreneurs may lack the practical experience, business acumen, and industry knowledge needed to navigate the complexities of entrepreneurship effectively. Understanding market dynamics, managing finances, and making strategic decisions can be daunting without prior experience.

Strategies: Seek opportunities for experiential learning, such as internships, part-time jobs, or volunteer work in relevant industries. Take advantage of entrepreneurship courses, workshops, and mentorship programs to gain valuable insights and skills.

Risk Aversion:

Students may be more risk-averse due to concerns about academic performance, financial stability, or societal expectations. Fear of failure or uncertainty about the future can inhibit entrepreneurial initiative and innovation.

Strategies: Cultivate an entrepreneurial mindset that embraces failure as a learning opportunity and views risk-taking as an essential part of the entrepreneurial journey. Develop resilience, perseverance, and adaptability to navigate setbacks and challenges with confidence.

Limited Network and Support System:

Building a robust network of mentors, advisors, peers, and collaborators is essential for student entrepreneurs. However, students may lack access to established networks or face challenges in building relationships and credibility in the business community.

Strategies: Actively seek out networking opportunities, attend entrepreneurship events, join student organizations, and engage with alumni networks to expand your circle of contacts. Be proactive in reaching out to potential mentors and advisors who can offer guidance, feedback, and support.

Academic Pressure:

Meeting academic requirements and maintaining good grades while pursuing entrepreneurial ventures can be demanding and stressful. The pressure to outshine academically may conflict with the time and energy needed to focus on business development.

Strategies: Communicate with professors and academic advisors about your entrepreneurial aspirations and seek their understanding and support. Look for opportunities to integrate entrepreneurial projects into coursework or leverage university resources for research, funding, or mentorship.

Regulatory and Legal Compliance:

Navigating regulatory requirements, legal obligations, and compliance standards can be daunting for student entrepreneurs, especially in highly regulated industries or complex legal environments.

Strategies: Educate yourself about relevant laws, regulations, and compliance requirements for your business. Seek guidance from legal experts, business advisors, or entrepreneurship centers to ensure that your venture operates ethically and legally.

Strategies for overcoming obstacles and setbacks

In the pursuit of entrepreneurship, obstacles and setbacks are inevitable. Whether it's facing financial challenges, encountering unexpected roadblocks, or dealing with failures, overcoming adversity is an integral part of the entrepreneurial journey. To navigate these challenges effectively and emerge stronger, entrepreneurs must employ strategies that foster resilience, innovation, and perseverance. Here are some key strategies for overcoming obstacles and setbacks in entrepreneurship:

Maintain a Positive Mindset:

Cultivate a positive and resilient mindset that sees obstacles as opportunities for growth and learning. Embrace setbacks as valuable lessons that provide insights, feedback, and opportunities for improvement.

Practice gratitude, self-reflection, and mindfulness to stay grounded and maintain perspective during difficult times. Surround yourself with positive influences and supportive peers who uplift and encourage you.

Adaptability and Flexibility:

Remain adaptable and flexible in the face of changing circumstances, market dynamics, and unexpected challenges. Be prepared to pivot your strategy, revise your plans, and explore alternative solutions as needed.

Embrace innovation and experimentation, viewing setbacks as opportunities to innovate, iterate, and evolve your business model or product offerings to better meet customer needs and market demands.

Seek Support and Guidance:

Don't hesitate to reach out for support and guidance when facing obstacles or setbacks. Build a strong support network of mentors, advisors, peers, and industry experts who can offer advice, insights, and encouragement.

Engage with entrepreneurship communities, networking events, and support groups to connect with like-minded individuals who understand the challenges of entrepreneurship and can provide valuable perspectives and resources.

Problem-Solving and Resourcefulness:

Approach obstacles with a problem solving mindset! Break down complex challenges into smaller, manageable tasks. Identify the root causes of problems and explore creative solutions that leverage your strengths and available resources.

Practice resourcefulness and resilience, finding innovative ways to overcome limitations, constraints, or setbacks. Look for opportunities to leverage existing assets, forge strategic partnerships, or tap into new markets or revenue streams.

Stay Committed to Your Vision:

Stay committed to your entrepreneurial vision and long-term goals, even in the face of adversity. Remind yourself of the reasons why you embarked on this journey and the impact you aspire to make in the world.

Use setbacks as fuel to reignite your passion and determination, reinforcing your belief in the value of your venture and your ability to overcome challenges and succeed against all odds.

Learn from Failure and Adapt:

Embrace failure as a natural part of the entrepreneurial process and an opportunity for growth and improvement. Analyze the root causes of failures, extract key lessons and insights, and apply them to future endeavors.

Adopt a continuous learning mindset, seeking feedback, acquiring new skills, and refining your approach based on past experiences and lessons learned. Use failures as stepping stones towards greater success and resilience.

Celebrate Small Wins and Progress:

Acknowledge and celebrate small victories, milestones, and progress along the way, no matter how minor they may seem. Recognize the effort, resilience, and perseverance required to overcome obstacles and setbacks.

Cultivate a culture of resilience and positivity within your team or organization, fostering camaraderie, motivation, and a shared sense of accomplishment in the face of adversity.

Handling time management and balancing academic and entrepreneurial commitments

As a student entrepreneur, managing academic responsibilities alongside entrepreneurial pursuits can be a challenging cum balancing act. Time management becomes paramount to juggling coursework, exams, business meetings, and startup endeavors effectively. By implementing strategic time management techniques and prioritization strategies, student entrepreneurs can optimize productivity, maintain focus, and achieve success in both academic and entrepreneurial realms. Some practical tips for handling time management and balancing academic and entrepreneurial commitments:

Set Clear Priorities:

Begin by identifying your priorities and objectives in both academic and entrepreneurial domains. Determine which tasks or activities are most important and align closely with your long-term goals.

Rank your priorities based on urgency, importance, and impact, allocating more time and attention to high-priority tasks that contribute directly to your academic and business success.

Create a Structured Schedule:

Develop a structured schedule or timetable that allocates dedicated time blocks for academic study, business activities, personal commitments, and self-care. Use digital calendars, planners, or scheduling apps to organize your time effectively.

Block out specific time slots for attending classes, studying, working on business projects, meeting with team members or clients, and engaging in extracurricular activities.

Practice Effective Time Blocking:

Implement time blocking techniques to focus on specific tasks or projects without distractions. Allocate uninterrupted blocks of time for deep work, problem-solving, or creative brainstorming sessions.

Break down larger tasks into smaller, manageable chunks and assign time blocks for each component to make progress consistently without feeling overwhelmed.

Use the Pomodoro Technique:

Experiment with the Pomodoro Technique, a time management method that involves working in short, focused bursts followed by brief breaks. Set a timer for 25 minutes of focused work, followed by a 5-minute break, and repeat the cycle.

This technique can help enhance productivity, maintain concentration, and prevent burnout by incorporating regular intervals of rest and rejuvenation into your study and work sessions.

Prioritize Essential Tasks:

Identify essential tasks or deadlines that cannot be postponed and prioritize them accordingly. Focus on completing critical assignments, exams, or business deliverables that have immediate implications for your academic or entrepreneurial success.

Learn to distinguish between urgent tasks that require immediate attention and important tasks that contribute to long-term goals, allocating your time and energy accordingly.

Practice Self-Discipline and Time Management:

Cultivate self-discipline and self-control to resist distractions, procrastination, and time-wasting activities. Set boundaries around time-consuming activities such as social media, entertainment, or non-essential commitments.

Develop effective time management habits, such as setting realistic goals, adhering to deadlines, and tracking your progress regularly. Hold yourself accountable for managing your time effectively and making productive use of each day.

Delegate and Collaborate:

Learn to delegate tasks and responsibilities whenever possible, whether it's academic assignments, business tasks, or administrative duties. Delegate tasks to team members, classmates, or virtual assistants to lighten your workload and focus on higher-priority activities.

Foster collaboration and teamwork by leveraging the strengths and expertise of others. Build a support network of classmates, colleagues, mentors, and advisors who can provide assistance, guidance, and feedback when needed.

Practice Self-Care and Work-Life Balance:

Prioritize self-care and well-being to avoid burnout and maintain overall health and happiness. Incorporate regular breaks, exercise, relaxation, and leisure activities into your schedule to recharge and rejuvenate.

Strive to achieve a healthy work-life balance by setting boundaries between academic, entrepreneurial, and personal life domains. Allocate time for hobbies, socializing, and spending quality time with friends and family to maintain perspective and fulfillment beyond work and study.

Chapter 9: Legal and Ethical Considerations

Embarking on the entrepreneurial journey as a student involves more than just developing a great business idea; it also requires understanding and complying with legal requirements and regulations. From business registration to intellectual property protection, navigating the legal landscape is essential to ensure that your venture operates legally and responsibly. These are the key legal considerations for starting a business as a student:

Business Structure:

Choose an appropriate legal structure for your business, such as a sole proprietorship, partnership, limited liability company (LLC), or corporation. Each structure has different implications for taxation, liability, and management.

Consider consulting with a legal advisor or business attorney to determine the most suitable structure based on your business goals, risk tolerance, and long-term plans.

Business Registration:

Register your business with the appropriate government authorities at the local, state, and federal levels. Obtain the necessary permits, licenses, and registrations required to operate legally in your jurisdiction.

Research the specific registration requirements for your type of business and industry, including zoning regulations, health and safety standards, and industry-specific licenses or certifications.

Tax Obligations:

Understand your tax obligations as a business owner, including income tax, sales tax, payroll tax, and any other applicable taxes. Familiarize yourself with tax filing deadlines, reporting requirements, and deductions available to small businesses.

Consider consulting with a tax professional or accountant to ensure compliance with tax laws and maximize tax efficiency for your business.

Intellectual Property Protection:

Protect your intellectual property (IP) assets, such as trademarks, copyrights, patents, and trade secrets, to safeguard your business's unique brand identity, inventions, and creative works.

Conduct a thorough IP audit to identify and register any trademarks or copyrights associated with your business name, logo, products, or services. Consider filing for patents to protect innovative inventions or processes.

Contracts and Agreements:

Draft and negotiate contracts and agreements that govern your business relationships with customers, suppliers, partners, contractors, and employees. Ensure that contracts are clear, enforceable, and compliant with relevant laws.

Seek legal advice when drafting or reviewing contracts to avoid misunderstandings, disputes, or legal liabilities down the line. Include provisions for dispute resolution, confidentiality, indemnification, and termination as needed.

Employment Law Compliance:

Familiarize yourself with employment laws and regulations governing hiring, wages, benefits, workplace safety, and termination practices. Understand your responsibilities as an employer and ensure compliance with fair labor standards.

Develop employee policies and procedures that adhere to employment laws and promote a positive work environment. Provide training and resources to employees to educate them about their rights and responsibilities.

Data Protection and Privacy:

Protect customer data and privacy by implementing robust data security measures and complying with data protection laws, such as the General Data Protection Regulation (GDPR) or the California Consumer Privacy Act (CCPA).

Develop a privacy policy that outlines how you collect, use, store, and protect personal information collected from customers or website visitors. Obtain explicit consent from individuals before collecting or processing their data.

Compliance with Industry Regulations:

Research on the industry specific regulations and compliance requirements that apply to your business including food safety standards, financial regulations, environmental regulations and healthcare laws.

Stay informed about changes in regulations and monitor industry developments to ensure ongoing compliance with evolving legal requirements. Seek professional guidance or industry associations for assistance in navigating complex regulatory landscapes.

Risk Management and Liability Protection:

Mitigate legal risks and liabilities by implementing risk management strategies, such as obtaining insurance coverage, creating legal disclaimers, and maintaining accurate records and documentation.

Consider forming a separate legal entity, such as an LLC or corporation, to shield personal assets from business liabilities and lawsuits. Consult with legal and financial advisors to determine the most appropriate risk management strategies for your business.

Ethical and Social Responsibility:

Operate your business with integrity, transparency, and ethical principles that prioritize the well-being of stakeholders, including customers, employees, suppliers, and the community.

Adhere to ethical business practices, corporate social responsibility (CSR) standards, and sustainability principles that align with your values and contribute positively to society and the environment.

Intellectual property considerations

Intellectual property (IP) plays a pivotal role in protecting the innovative ideas, creations, and assets of student entrepreneurs. Whether it's a groundbreaking invention, a unique brand identity, or original creative works, safeguarding intellectual property rights is essential for preserving competitive advantage, fostering innovation, and ensuring long-term business success. Let's explore the key intellectual property considerations for student entrepreneurs:

Identify and Protect Your Intellectual Property:

Identify the intellectual property assets associated with your business, including trademarks, copyrights, patents, trade secrets, and domain names. Assess the uniqueness and value of each asset in relation to your business goals and market positioning.

Take proactive steps to protect your intellectual property through registration, documentation, and enforcement mechanisms. File for trademarks to protect your brand name, logos, and slogans; register copyrights for original creative works; and apply for patents to safeguard inventions or innovations.

Trademark Protection for Brand Identity:

Secure trademark protection for your business name, logo, and other brand elements to establish exclusive rights to use them in commerce. Conduct a trademark search to ensure that your chosen brand name is available and not already in use by others.

File a trademark application with the relevant government authority, such as the United States Patent and Trademark Office (USPTO), to register your trademarks and prevent unauthorized use by competitors or infringers.

Copyright Protection for Creative Works:

Obtain copyright protection for original creative works, such as written content, artwork, designs, software code, and multimedia productions. Copyright automatically applies to creative works upon their creation, but registration provides additional legal benefits and enforcement options.

Register your copyrights with the U.S. Copyright Office to establish a public record of ownership and eligibility for statutory damages and attorney's fees in case of infringement disputes.

Patent Protection for Inventions and Innovations:

Consider seeking patent protection for novel inventions, processes, or technologies that offer a competitive advantage in the marketplace. A patent grants exclusive rights to make, use, or sell the patented invention for a limited period, typically 20 years from the filing date.

Conduct a prior art search to assess the patentability and novelty of your invention before filing a patent application. Work with a patent attorney or agent to draft and file a patent application that meets the legal requirements and maximizes the scope of protection.

Trade Secret Protection for Confidential Information:

Safeguard trade secrets, proprietary information, and confidential business data through appropriate measures such as non-disclosure agreements (NDAs), employee training, and access controls. Trade secrets can include formulas, algorithms, customer lists, and manufacturing processes that provide a competitive advantage.

Implement policies and procedures to protect trade secrets from unauthorized access, disclosure, or misappropriation, both within your organization and when sharing information with third parties.

Domain Name Protection and Brand Enforcement:

Secure domain name registrations that reflect your business name, brand, or trademark to establish an online presence and prevent cybersquatting or brand impersonation. Register variations of your domain name to protect your online brand identity and prevent confusion among customers.

Monitor the internet for unauthorized use of your trademarks or copyrighted materials and take prompt action to enforce your intellectual property rights. Send cease-and-desist letters, file complaints with domain registrars or hosting providers, and pursue legal remedies against infringers.

Intellectual Property Licensing and Commercialization:

Explore opportunities to monetize your intellectual property through licensing, franchising, or strategic partnerships. License your trademarks, copyrights, or patents to third parties in exchange for royalties, licensing fees, or other forms of compensation.

Negotiate licensing agreements that define the terms and conditions of use, quality standards, royalty payments, and enforcement mechanisms to protect your intellectual property rights and preserve your brand integrity.

Stay Informed and Seek Professional Guidance:

Stay informed about developments in intellectual property law, industry trends, and best practices for IP protection and enforcement. Monitor changes in regulations, court decisions, and international treaties that may impact your intellectual property rights.

Seek guidance from legal professionals, such as intellectual property attorneys, patent agents, or trademark specialists, to navigate the complexities of IP law and develop a comprehensive IP strategy tailored to your business objectives and circumstances.

Ethical business practices

In the dynamic landscape of entrepreneurship, ethical business practices serve as guiding principles that foster trust, integrity, and sustainability. As student entrepreneurs, embracing ethical conduct is not only a moral imperative but also a strategic advantage that contributes to long-term success, reputation building, and stakeholder trust. Let's look at the fundamental principles and best practices of ethical business conduct for student entrepreneurs:

Integrity and Honesty:

Conduct business with honesty, integrity, and transparency in all interactions with customers, employees, suppliers, and other stakeholders. Uphold high ethical standards and adhere to the principles of truthfulness, fairness, and accountability.

Avoid misleading or deceptive practices, such as false advertising, misrepresentation of products or services, or omitting relevant information that could impact stakeholders' decisions.

Respect for Stakeholders:

Treat all stakeholders with respect, dignity, and fairness, regardless of their background, beliefs, or status. Value diversity, inclusivity, and equal opportunity in your business practices and relationships.

Foster a culture of mutual respect, open communication, and collaboration that values the contributions and perspectives of all stakeholders, including employees, customers, suppliers, and community members.

Customer Focus and Satisfaction:

Prioritize customer satisfaction and strive to exceed customer expectations by delivering high-quality products, exceptional service, and positive experiences. Listen to customer feedback, address concerns promptly, and continuously improve your offerings based on customer needs and preferences.

Build long-term relationships with customers based on trust, loyalty, and reliability, rather than short-term gains or transactional interactions.

Fair Treatment of Employees:

Provide a safe, healthy, and inclusive work environment that promotes employee well-being, professional development, and work-life balance. Respect employee rights, including fair wages, equal opportunities, and freedom from discrimination or harassment.

Foster a culture of fairness, teamwork, and meritocracy that recognizes and rewards employees' contributions, encourages diversity of thought, and empowers individuals to reach their full potential.

Environmental Responsibility:

Embrace environmental sustainability and responsibility in your business practices, operations, and supply chain management.

Minimize your environmental footprint by adopting eco-friendly practices, reducing waste, and conserving natural resources.

Consider the environmental impact of your business activities and seek opportunities to implement green initiatives, renewable energy solutions, and sustainable business practices that contribute to environmental preservation and climate action.

Ethical Leadership and Decision-Making:

Lead by example and demonstrate ethical leadership in all aspects of your business operations and decision-making. Set clear ethical standards, communicate your values and expectations, and hold yourself and others accountable for upholding ethical principles.

Consider the ethical implications of your decisions and actions, weighing the potential impact on stakeholders, society, and the environment. Seek input from trusted advisors, mentors, or ethical frameworks to guide your decision-making process.

Compliance with Laws and Regulations:

Ensure compliance with applicable laws, regulations, and industry standards governing your business activities, products, and services. Stay informed about the changes in legal requirements and maintain diligent records and documentation to demonstrate compliance.

Develop policies, procedures, and internal controls to prevent unethical behavior, mitigate legal risks, and promote a culture of legal and regulatory compliance within your organization.

Community Engagement and Social Responsibility:

Give back to the community and support social causes through philanthropy, volunteerism, or corporate social responsibility (CSR) initiatives. Engage with local communities, nonprofit organizations, and social impact initiatives to make a positive difference and contribute to societal well-being.

Align your business practices with ethical and social values that promote social justice, equity, and human rights. Consider the broader social and ethical implications of your business decisions and seek to create shared value for all stakeholders.

Continuous Improvement and Accountability:

Commit to continuous improvement and self-reflection as a student entrepreneur, seeking feedback, learning from mistakes, and striving to do better. Embrace a growth mindset that values learning, adaptability, and innovation.

Hold yourself and your business accountable for ethical conduct, transparency, and responsible business practices. Establish mechanisms for feedback, reporting, and accountability to address ethical concerns or violations promptly and effectively.

Chapter 10: Launching and Scaling Your Business

Embarking on the journey of entrepreneurship as a student can be an exhilarating and rewarding experience. From refining your business idea to executing your launch strategy, each step of the process plays a crucial role in turning your vision into reality. To guide you through the exhilarating process, here's a step-by-step guide to launching your business:

Define Your Business Idea:

Start by clarifying your business concept and identifying the problem you aim to solve or the opportunity you wish to seize. Consider your passions, skills, and market trends to refine your business idea and differentiate it from competitors.

Conduct Market Research:

Validate your business idea through market research to understand your target audience, customer needs, and competitive landscape. Gather insights from surveys, interviews, and industry reports to assess market demand and identify opportunities for innovation.

Develop a Business Plan:

Create a comprehensive business plan that outlines your business objectives, target market, value proposition, revenue model, marketing strategy, and financial projections. Use templates or tools to structure your plan and ensure it is realistic and actionable.

Secure Funding or Resources:

Determine your startup costs and financial needs, and explore funding options such as personal savings, bootstrapping, loans, grants, or investment from family and friends. Develop a budget and financial plan to allocate resources effectively and sustainably.

Choose a Legal Structure:

Select an appropriate legal structure for your business, such as a sole proprietorship, partnership, limited liability company (LLC), or corporation. Consider factors like liability protection, tax implications, and administrative requirements when choosing your structure.

Register Your Business:

Register your business with the relevant government authorities at the local, state, and federal levels. Obtain the necessary permits, licenses, and registrations required to operate legally in your jurisdiction.

Build Your Brand:

Develop your brand identity, including your business name, logo, colors, and messaging. Create a compelling brand story that resonates with your target audience and communicates your values, mission, and unique selling proposition.

Create a Minimum Viable Product (MVP):

Develop a prototype or minimum viable product (MVP) to test your business concept and gather feedback from early adopters. Focus on delivering core features and functionalities that address the most pressing customer needs or pain points.

Launch Your Marketing Campaign:

Plan and execute a marketing campaign to generate awareness and attract customers to your business. Utilize a mix of online and offline channels, such as social media, email marketing, content marketing, SEO, advertising, and networking events.

Establish Operations and Infrastructure:

Set up the necessary infrastructure and operational processes to support your business activities, such as setting up a website, establishing a physical location, hiring employees, sourcing suppliers, and managing inventory.

Deliver Exceptional Customer Experience:

Prioritize customer satisfaction and deliver exceptional experiences at every touchpoint of the customer journey. Provide personalized service, listen to customer feedback, and address concerns promptly to build trust and loyalty.

Monitor Performance and Iterate:

Track key performance indicators (KPIs) and metrics to measure the success of your business and identify areas for improvement. Continuously iterate and refine your strategies based on data-driven insights and customer feedback.

Adapt and Innovate:

Stay agile and adaptable in response to changing market conditions, customer preferences, and industry trends. Embrace innovation and experimentation to stay ahead of the competition and seize new opportunities for growth.

Seek Mentorship and Support:

Surround yourself with mentors, advisors, and peers who can provide guidance, support, and valuable insights throughout your entrepreneurial journey. Join entrepreneurship programs, incubators, or networking groups to connect with like-minded individuals and access resources and opportunities.

Celebrate Milestones and Successes:

Take time to celebrate milestones, achievements, and successes along the way, no matter how small. Acknowledge the hard work, dedication, and perseverance that have brought you this far and use these moments as motivation to keep moving forward.

Strategies for gaining initial traction and acquiring customers

As a student entrepreneur, gaining initial traction and acquiring customers are critical milestones on the path to success. Building awareness, generating interest, and converting prospects into loyal customers require strategic planning, creativity, and relentless execution. Here are some effective strategies for gaining traction and acquiring your first customers:

Define Your Target Audience:

Clearly define your target market and ideal customer profile based on demographics, psychographics, and behavioral traits. Understand their needs, pain points, and preferences to tailor your marketing messages and offerings accordingly.

Create Compelling Value Proposition:

Develop a compelling value proposition that communicates the unique benefits and value your product or service offers to customers. Highlight how your solution solves their problems, fulfills their desires, or improves their lives in meaningful ways.

Utilize Digital Marketing Channels:

Leverage digital marketing channels such as social media, content marketing, email marketing, search engine optimization (SEO), and paid advertising to reach and engage your target audience online. Develop a multi-channel marketing strategy that combines different tactics to maximize reach and impact.

Build an Online Presence:

Establish a professional and user-friendly website that showcases your brand, products, and value proposition. Optimize your website for search engines and mobile devices to improve visibility and accessibility to potential customers.

Engage in Content Marketing:

Create valuable, informative, and engaging content that educates, entertains, or inspires your target audience. Publish blog posts, articles, videos, podcasts, or infographics that address their pain points, answer their questions, or provide solutions to their problems.

Leverage Social Media:

Build a strong presence on social media platforms relevant to your target audience, such as Facebook, Instagram, Twitter, LinkedIn, or TikTok. Share engaging content, interact with followers, and participate in relevant conversations to increase brand visibility and engagement.

Offer Incentives and Promotions:

Attract new customers by offering incentives, discounts, or promotions to encourage them to try your products or services. Consider offering limited-time offers, referral bonuses, or exclusive deals to incentivize purchases and drive conversion.

Harness the Power of Influencers:

Collaborate with influencers, bloggers, or industry experts who have a relevant and engaged audience aligned with your target market. Partner with influencers to promote your brand, endorse your products, or share authentic testimonials and reviews.

Attend Networking Events and Trade Shows:

Participate in networking events, industry conferences, trade shows, or startup competitions to connect with potential customers, partners, and investors. Use these opportunities to showcase your products, demo your offerings, and build relationships with key stakeholders.

Offer Exceptional Customer Experience:

Focus on delivering exceptional customer service and experiences that exceed customer expectations. Provide personalized support, address customer inquiries promptly, and go above and beyond to delight customers at every touchpoint.

Implement Referral Programs:

Cheer up the satisfied customers to refer their friends, family, or colleagues to your business through referral programs or incentives. Offer rewards, discounts, or exclusive perks for successful referrals to incentivize word-of-mouth marketing and customer advocacy.

Collect and Utilize Customer Feedback:

Gather feedback from customers through surveys, reviews, and testimonials to understand their satisfaction levels, preferences, and areas for improvement. Use customer feedback to refine your products, optimize your marketing strategies, and enhance the overall customer experience.

Monitor and Analyze Performance Metrics:

Track key performance indicators (KPIs) and metrics related to customer acquisition, engagement, and retention. Monitor metrics such as website traffic, conversion rates, customer acquisition cost (CAC), and customer lifetime value (CLV) to assess the effectiveness of your marketing efforts and optimize your strategies accordingly.

Iterate and Experiment:

Continuously iterate and experiment with different marketing tactics, messaging, and channels to identify what resonates most with your target audience. Be open to testing new ideas, learning from failures, and adapting your approach based on data-driven insights and customer feedback.

Stay Persistent and Resilient:

Building traction and acquiring customers takes time, effort, and persistence. Stay committed to your goals, stay resilient in the face of challenges, and remain adaptable to changing market conditions. Keep experimenting, learning, and refining your strategies until you find what works best for your business.

Scaling your business while managing academic responsibilities

Scaling a business is an exciting but challenging endeavor, especially for student entrepreneurs juggling academic commitments alongside their entrepreneurial pursuits. Successfully growing your venture while balancing the demands of coursework, exams, and other academic responsibilities requires careful planning, prioritization, and effective time management. Here are some strategies to help you scale your business while managing your academic workload:

Set Clear Goals and Priorities:

Define clear goals and priorities for both your academic and entrepreneurial endeavors. Identify the key milestones you aim to achieve in your business growth and academic performance, and allocate time and resources accordingly.

Optimize Your Schedule:

Develop a structured schedule or timetable that accommodates both your academic and business activities. Block out dedicated time slots for attending classes, studying, working on your business, and other commitments.

Prioritize tasks based on urgency, importance, and impact, and allocate focused blocks of time for high-priority activities that contribute to your long-term goals.

Leverage Technology and Automation:

Use technology tools and automation software to streamline repetitive tasks, improve efficiency, and save time. Explore productivity apps, project management tools, and communication platforms that help you manage your workload more effectively.

Automate routine processes such as scheduling appointments, sending email reminders, or managing social media accounts to free up time for higher-value tasks.

Delegate and Outsource:

Delegate non-essential tasks or responsibilities to trusted team members, classmates, or virtual assistants. Identify areas where you can outsource tasks such as administrative work, marketing, or customer support to focus on core activities.

Build a reliable support network of collaborators, freelancers, or interns who can help you manage workload peaks, meet deadlines, and maintain productivity during busy periods.

Focus on High-Impact Activities:

Prioritize high-impact activities that drive business growth and academic success. Invest your time and energy in tasks that have the greatest potential to generate revenue, acquire customers, or advance your academic goals.

Delegate or eliminate low-value tasks that do not contribute significantly to your objectives, and focus on activities that align with your priorities and long-term vision.

Practice Effective Time Management:

Implement time management techniques such as the Pomodoro Technique, time blocking, or the Eisenhower Matrix to structure your time and maximize productivity. Break down tasks into manageable chunks and allocate specific time blocks for focused work.

Set realistic goals and deadlines for completing academic assignments and business projects, and use time tracking tools to monitor your progress and stay on track.

Maintain Work-Life Balance:

Prioritize self-care and well-being to avoid burnout and maintain balance between your academic and entrepreneurial pursuits. Allocate time for relaxation, exercise, hobbies, and social activities to recharge and rejuvenate.

Set boundaries between work and personal life, and establish designated times for work, study, and leisure to ensure that you maintain a healthy balance and avoid excessive stress or fatigue.

Communicate and Negotiate Flexibility:

Communicate openly with your professors, classmates, and team members about your academic and business commitments. Seek their understanding and support, and negotiate flexibility or accommodations when necessary to balance conflicting demands.

Be proactive in managing expectations and communicating your availability, deadlines, and priorities to ensure that everyone is aligned and aware of your commitments.

Stay Agile and Adaptive:

Embrace agility and adaptability in response to changing circumstances, priorities, and opportunities. Be prepared to adjust your plans, strategies, and timelines based on feedback, new information, or unexpected challenges.

Continuously monitor your progress, evaluate your strategies, and iterate your approach to optimize your performance and adapt to evolving academic and business environments.

Seek Mentorship and Guidance:

Seek guidance and mentorship from experienced entrepreneurs, professors, or advisors who can provide valuable insights, advice, and support. Learn from their experiences, seek their feedback on your ideas and strategies, and leverage their expertise to navigate challenges and make informed decisions.

Celebrate Milestones and Achievements:

Celebrate your accomplishments and milestones in both your academic and entrepreneurial journey. Acknowledge your progress, recognize your achievements, and take pride in your ability to balance multiple responsibilities and pursue your passions.

Chapter 11: Case Studies and Success Stories

In the world of student entrepreneurship, there are countless inspiring stories of ambitious individuals who have turned their innovative ideas into thriving businesses while still pursuing their academic goals. These case studies and success stories offer valuable insights, lessons learned, and motivation for aspiring student entrepreneurs. Let's explore a few notable examples:

Dropbox:

Founded by Drew Houston and Arash Ferdowsi while they were students at MIT, Dropbox is a cloud storage and file-sharing service that has revolutionized the way people store, access, and share their files. The idea for Dropbox was born out of Houston's frustration with forgetting his USB drive while traveling, leading him to create a solution for easily accessing files from anywhere.

Despite facing initial skepticism and competition in the crowded tech market, Dropbox gained traction through a combination of clever marketing tactics, a user-friendly product design, and strategic partnerships. Today, Dropbox boasts millions of users worldwide and has become a household name in cloud storage.

Facebook:

Mark Zuckerberg famously launched Facebook from his Harvard dorm room along with his college roommates, Dustin Moskovitz, Eduardo Saverin, and Chris Hughes. Initially conceived as a social networking platform for Harvard students, Facebook quickly expanded to other universities and eventually became a global phenomenon.

Through relentless iteration, user feedback, and strategic expansion, Facebook evolved from a college campus network into the world's largest social media platform, connecting billions of people around the globe. Zuckerberg's visionary leadership and unwavering determination propelled Facebook to become one of the most influential companies of the 21st century.

Spanx:

Sara Blakely, a former door-to-door fax machine salesperson, founded Spanx in 2000 with just $5,000 in savings. Blakely's innovative idea for footless pantyhose was inspired by her own desire for a more flattering and comfortable undergarment. Despite facing plentiful rejections from potential investors and manufacturers, Blakely persisted and eventually launched Spanx as a direct-to-consumer brand.

Through savvy marketing, word-of-mouth buzz, and celebrity endorsements, Spanx quickly gained a cult following and became synonymous with shapewear and body confidence. Blakely's entrepreneurial journey from humble beginnings to becoming the world's youngest self-made female billionaire is a testament to her resilience, creativity, and entrepreneurial spirit.

Reddit:

Founded by Steve Huffman and Alexis Ohanian while they were students at the University of Virginia, Reddit is a social news aggregation and discussion platform that has become one of the most popular websites on the internet. The idea for Reddit was inspired by Huffman and Ohanian's shared interest in internet communities and online discussion forums.

Despite facing technical challenges and limited resources, Huffman and Ohanian bootstrapped Reddit's development and launched the platform in 2005. Through grassroots marketing efforts and a commitment to user engagement and community building, Reddit quickly gained momentum and grew into a global hub for discussion, debate, and sharing of content.

Warby Parker:

Warby Parker was founded by four students from the Wharton School of the University of Pennsylvania—Neil Blumenthal, Andrew Hunt, David Gilboa, and Jeffrey Raider. The idea for Warby Parker emerged from the founders' frustration with the high cost of eyewear and lack of stylish, affordable options.

By disrupting the traditional eyewear industry with a direct-to-consumer model and a socially conscious mission, Warby Parker quickly gained a loyal following and disrupted the eyewear industry. Through innovative marketing, a seamless online shopping experience, and a commitment to social impact, Warby Parker has become a leading eyewear brand known for its affordability, style, and social responsibility.

Chapter 12: Resources and Tools for Student Entrepreneurs

For student entrepreneurs seeking to enhance their knowledge, skills, and entrepreneurial mindset, there is a wealth of resources available in the form of books, websites, and online courses. Whether you're looking to learn about startup strategies, business development, marketing techniques, or personal growth, these curated resources provide valuable insights and practical guidance to support your entrepreneurial journey. Here are some recommended books, websites, and online courses for student entrepreneurs:

Books:

"The Lean Startup" by Eric Ries:

This groundbreaking book introduces the principles of lean startup methodology, emphasizing rapid experimentation, validated learning, and iterative product development. Ideal for aspiring entrepreneurs looking to build and scale successful startups in a fast-changing business landscape.

"Zero to One" by Peter Thiel:

Written by PayPal co-founder and venture capitalist Peter Thiel, this book offers contrarian insights on entrepreneurship, innovation, and creating value in the digital age. Thiel shares his perspectives on building transformative companies that go from zero to becoming monopolies in their industries.

"Start with Why" by Simon Sinek:

Simon Sinek explores the concept of purpose-driven leadership and the importance of defining your "why" in business and life. This book inspires entrepreneurs to uncover their core values, mission, and vision to drive meaningful impact and build successful ventures.

"The $100 Startup" by Chris Guillebeau:

Offering practical advice and inspiring case studies, this book shows how ordinary people can start small businesses with minimal investment and turn their passion into profit. Guillebeau highlights the stories of entrepreneurs who have achieved success by following their dreams and taking calculated risks.

"Crushing It!: How Great Entrepreneurs Build Their Business and Influence—and How You Can, Too" by Gary Vaynerchuk:

Entrepreneur and social media expert Gary Vaynerchuk shares strategies for leveraging social media platforms to build personal brands, grow businesses, and create meaningful connections with audiences. Packed with actionable insights and real-world examples, this book empowers entrepreneurs to crush it in their respective industries.

Websites:

Entrepreneur.com:

Entrepreneur.com is a leading online resource for entrepreneurship news, insights, and advice. From startup guides and business ideas to industry trends and success stories, Entrepreneur.com offers a wealth of articles, videos, and resources to help student entrepreneurs navigate the challenges of starting and growing a business.

Inc.com:

Inc.com provides a wide range of articles, tools, and resources for startup founders and small business owners. Explore topics such as leadership, marketing, finance, and innovation, and gain valuable insights from interviews with successful entrepreneurs and thought leaders.

StartupNation.com:

StartupNation.com is a comprehensive platform for aspiring entrepreneurs, offering practical advice, step-by-step guides, and community support. Discover resources on business planning, funding, marketing, and operations, and connect with fellow entrepreneurs through forums, podcasts, and events.

Udemy.com:

Udemy is an online learning platform that offers a diverse range of courses on entrepreneurship, business development, marketing, and personal growth. Explore courses taught by industry experts and thought leaders, and learn at your own pace from anywhere in the world.

Coursera.org:

Coursera partners with top universities and institutions to offer courses, specializations, and online degrees on entrepreneurship, innovation, and business strategy. Enroll in courses taught by professors from institutions like Stanford University, Wharton School of the University of Pennsylvania, and Harvard University, and gain valuable skills and knowledge to fuel your entrepreneurial journey.

Online Courses:

"Startup School" by Y Combinator:

Y Combinator's Startup School is a free online course that provides practical advice, mentorship, and resources for startup founders. Join a global community of entrepreneurs, participate in weekly lectures and workshops, and receive personalized feedback and support from experienced mentors.

"How to Start a Startup" by Sam Altman and the Stanford University team:

This series of lectures, hosted by Y Combinator president Sam Altman and featuring guest speakers from leading tech companies, provides insights into the key principles and strategies for building successful startups. Learn from the experiences of startup founders, investors, and industry experts as they share their insights on topics such as idea generation, product development, and fundraising.

"Marketing in a Digital World" by the University of Illinois at Urbana-Champaign (Coursera):

This course explores the fundamentals of digital marketing and how to leverage digital channels to reach and engage customers effectively. Learn about topics such as social media marketing, content strategy, search engine optimization (SEO), and data analytics to drive growth and awareness for your business.

"Financial Accounting Fundamentals" by the University of Virginia (Coursera):

Gain a foundational understanding of financial accounting principles and practices essential for managing finances and making informed business decisions. Learn how to read and interpret financial statements, analyze financial performance, and assess the financial health of your business.

"Leadership and Influence" by the University of Michigan (Coursera):

This course explores the principles of effective leadership and influence, with a focus on developing leadership skills, building high-performing teams, and fostering a culture of innovation and collaboration. Learn how to inspire and motivate others, navigate complex challenges, and lead with authenticity and integrity.

Networking opportunities and entrepreneurship organizations for students

Networking is a vital aspect of entrepreneurship, offering students valuable opportunities to connect with like-minded individuals, mentors, investors, and industry experts who can provide guidance, support, and opportunities for collaboration. Fortunately, there are numerous networking opportunities and entrepreneurship organizations tailored specifically for students looking to expand their professional network, gain insights, and accelerate their entrepreneurial journey. Here are some recommended networking opportunities and organizations for student entrepreneurs:

1. University Entrepreneurship Clubs:

Many universities and colleges have entrepreneurship clubs or organizations dedicated to fostering entrepreneurial spirit and supporting student startups. These clubs often host networking events, workshops, pitch competitions, and mentorship programs, providing students with opportunities to connect with peers, alumni, and industry professionals.

2. Startup Accelerators and Incubators:

Joining a startup accelerator or incubator program can provide access to a vibrant entrepreneurial community, mentorship from experienced entrepreneurs and investors, and resources to help accelerate your startup's growth. Look for accelerator programs specifically designed for student founders, such as those affiliated with universities or entrepreneurship hubs.

3. Hackathons and Startup Competitions:

Participating in hackathons, startup competitions, and innovation challenges can be a great way to network with other students, developers, designers, and entrepreneurs while gaining hands-on experience in problem-solving and innovation. These events often attract participants from diverse backgrounds and disciplines, fostering creativity and collaboration.

4. Industry Networking Events and Conferences:

Attend industry-specific networking events, conferences, and trade shows related to your area of interest or expertise. These events provide opportunities to meet professionals, investors, and potential partners in your industry, learn about the latest trends and innovations, and showcase your startup to a broader audience.

5. Online Communities and Forums:

Join online communities, forums, and social media groups focused on entrepreneurship, startups, and specific industries or interests. Platforms like LinkedIn, Reddit, and Facebook offer opportunities to connect with fellow entrepreneurs, share knowledge, ask questions, and seek advice from experienced professionals.

6. Alumni Networks:

Leverage your university's alumni network to connect with graduates who have pursued entrepreneurial ventures or work in relevant industries. Alumni can offer valuable insights, mentorship, and networking opportunities, as well as potential funding or partnership opportunities for your startup.

7. Entrepreneurship Conferences and Summits:

Attend entrepreneurship conferences, summits, and networking events organized by industry associations, startup accelerators, or professional organizations. These events feature keynote speakers, panel discussions, workshops, and networking sessions where you can learn from experts, connect with peers, and gain inspiration for your entrepreneurial journey.

8. Online Platforms and Communities:

Explore online platforms and communities dedicated to entrepreneurship and innovation, such as StartupGrind, Founder Institute, and AngelList. These platforms offer resources, networking opportunities, and connections to investors, mentors, and potential collaborators from around the world.

9. Guest Lectures and Workshops:

Take advantage of guest lectures, workshops, and seminars hosted by your university's entrepreneurship center, business school, or innovation hub. These events often feature successful entrepreneurs, industry leaders, and subject matter experts who share insights, experiences, and advice on various aspects of entrepreneurship.

10. Local Meetups and Networking Groups:

- Join local entrepreneurship meetups, networking groups, and co-working spaces in your area to connect with fellow entrepreneurs, freelancers, and small business owners. These informal gatherings provide opportunities to exchange ideas, build relationships, and find potential collaborators or mentors within your local community.

Tools and software to streamline business operations

Efficiently managing business operations is essential for student entrepreneurs striving to balance academic responsibilities with the demands of running a startup. Leveraging the right tools and software can streamline processes, improve productivity, and enhance collaboration, allowing you to focus on growing your business while maximizing your time and resources. Here are some essential tools and software solutions tailored for student entrepreneurs:

Project Management:

Trello: A visual project management tool that helps you organize tasks, collaborate with team members, and track progress using customizable boards and cards.

Asana: A versatile project management platform that allows you to create and assign tasks, set deadlines, and monitor project timelines and milestones.

Communication and Collaboration:

Slack: A team communication tool that facilitates real-time messaging, file sharing, and collaboration across teams and channels.

Microsoft Teams: A unified communication and collaboration platform that integrates chat, video conferencing, file storage, and project management features.

Document Management:

Google Workspace (formerly G Suite): A suite of productivity tools including Gmail, Google Drive, Docs, Sheets, and Slides for email, document creation, collaboration, and storage.

Microsoft Office 365: A cloud-based suite of productivity tools including Outlook, OneDrive, Word, Excel, and PowerPoint for communication, document management, and collaboration.

Financial Management:

QuickBooks Online: An accounting software solution that helps you track expenses, manage invoices, reconcile transactions, and generate financial reports.

Wave: A free accounting and invoicing platform designed for small businesses and freelancers, offering features such as invoicing, accounting, and receipt scanning.

Customer Relationship Management (CRM):

HubSpot CRM: A free CRM platform that allows you to manage contacts, track interactions, and nurture leads through the sales funnel.

Salesforce Essentials: A scalable CRM solution designed for small businesses, offering features such as contact management, opportunity tracking, and sales forecasting.

Email Marketing:

Mailchimp: An email marketing platform that enables you to create, send, and track email campaigns, automate workflows, and analyze campaign performance.

Constant Contact: An email marketing and automation platform that helps you engage subscribers, segment lists, and drive conversions through targeted campaigns.

Social Media Management:

Hootsuite: A social media management platform that allows you to schedule posts, monitor mentions, analyze performance, and engage with your audience across multiple social networks.

Buffer: A simple yet powerful social media scheduling tool that enables you to plan, publish, and analyze posts across various social media platforms.

Website and E-commerce:

WordPress: A popular content management system (CMS) that allows you to build and customize websites using themes and plugins, with options for blogging, e-commerce, and more.

Shopify: An all-in-one e-commerce platform that enables you to create and customize online stores, manage products, process orders, and track sales.

Analytics and Data Visualization:

Google Analytics: A web analytics service that provides insights into website traffic, user behavior, and conversion metrics, helping you make data-driven decisions to optimize performance.

Tableau Public: A data visualization tool that allows you to produce interactive charts, graphs, and dashboards to explore and share insights from your data.

Cybersecurity and Data Protection:

LastPass: A password management tool that securely stores and manages passwords, simplifying access to accounts and protecting against unauthorized access.

Norton 360: An all-in-one cybersecurity solution that offers antivirus protection, VPN, device security, and identity theft protection for your devices and online activities.

Conclusion

As student entrepreneurs, embarking on the journey of building a business while managing academic responsibilities requires careful planning, perseverance, and a commitment to continuous learning and growth. Throughout this guide, we've explored various aspects of entrepreneurship and provided practical insights, strategies, and resources to support you on your entrepreneurial journey. Let's recap some of the key points covered:

Refining Your Business Idea:

Start by identifying problems or opportunities aligned with your interests, skills, and market demand.

Conduct thorough market research to validate your idea and understand your target audience's needs and preferences.

Creating a Unique Value Proposition:

Develop a compelling value proposition that differentiates your business from competitors and resonates with your target customers.

Communicate your unique selling points clearly and effectively to attract and retain customers.

Prototyping and Testing Your Business Concept:

Build a minimum viable product (MVP) to test your idea and gather feedback from early adopters.

Iterate and refine your product or service based on user feedback and market validation.

Writing a Comprehensive Business Plan:

Develop a detailed business plan outlining your objectives, target market, value proposition, marketing strategy, and financial projections.

Use your business plan as a roadmap to guide your decision-making and communicate your vision to stakeholders.

Setting SMART Goals and Mission Statement:

Establish clear, measurable, achievable, relevant, and time-bound (SMART) goals to track your progress and drive accountability.

Write a mission statement that articulates your company's purpose, values, and long-term vision.

Financial Planning and Budgeting:

Develop a financial plan that outlines your startup costs, revenue projections, and cash flow forecasts.

Budget wisely and allocate resources strategically to ensure sustainable growth and profitability.

Overcoming Challenges and Setbacks:

Anticipate and prepare for common challenges faced by student entrepreneurs, such as time management, funding constraints, and academic commitments.

Stay resilient, adaptable, and resourceful in overcoming obstacles and setbacks along the way.

Understanding Legal and Intellectual Property Considerations:

Familiarize yourself with the legal requirements for starting a business, including business registration, permits, and licenses.

Protect your intellectual property through trademarks, patents, copyrights, and non-disclosure agreements (NDAs) to safeguard your ideas and innovations.

Embracing Ethical Business Practices:

Conduct business with integrity, honesty, and transparency, and prioritize the well-being of your customers, employees, and stakeholders.

Adhere to ethical standards and values that reflect positively on your brand and reputation.

Networking Opportunities and Entrepreneurship Organizations:

Take advantage of networking opportunities, entrepreneurship clubs, and organizations to connect with peers, mentors, and industry professionals.

Join online communities, attend events, and participate in hackathons to expand your network and access valuable resources and support.

As you embark on your entrepreneurial journey as a student, remember that success is not only measured by financial gains or business growth but also by your personal growth, resilience, and impact on others. Stay curious, stay hungry for knowledge, and stay committed to pursuing your dreams with passion and purpose. With dedication, perseverance, and a growth mindset, you have the potential to create meaningful change and make a lasting impact in the world of entrepreneurship.

A dose of motivation

To the aspiring student entrepreneurs out there,

Embarking on the journey of entrepreneurship as a student is an exciting and rewarding endeavor filled with limitless possibilities. As you navigate the challenges of balancing academic responsibilities with the pursuit of your entrepreneurial dreams, remember that every obstacle you encounter is an opportunity for growth and learning. Here's some motivation to fuel your entrepreneurial journey:

You Have the Power to Make a Difference:

As a student entrepreneur, you possess the creativity, passion, and drive to make a meaningful impact in the world. Whether you're solving a pressing problem, innovating in a specific industry, or creating opportunities for others, your ideas and actions have the power to inspire change and leave a lasting legacy.

Embrace Your Unique Perspective:

Your experiences as a student give you a unique perspective and fresh insights that can drive innovation and disrupt industries. Embrace your youth, curiosity, and willingness to challenge the status quo, and use your perspective to identify new opportunities and forge your own path in the entrepreneurial landscape.

Failure is a Stepping Stone to Success:

Failure is not the end but rather a stepping stone on the path to success. Embrace failure as a valuable learning experience, a source of resilience, and a catalyst for growth. Every setback you encounter brings you one step closer to achieving your goals and realizing your full potential as an entrepreneur.

You Are Not Alone:

Remember that you are not alone on your entrepreneurial journey. Seek guidance, support, and mentorship from fellow students, faculty members, alumni, and members of the entrepreneurial community. Surround yourself with positive influences, collaborators, and mentors who believe in your vision and are committed to helping you succeed.

Stay Focused on Your Why:

Stay true to your passion, purpose, and vision as you navigate the ups and downs of entrepreneurship. Clarify your "why" – the driving force behind your entrepreneurial journey – and let it guide your decisions, actions, and priorities. When faced with challenges or setbacks, remind yourself of your purpose and stay focused on the impact you aspire to create.

Celebrate Every Success, Big or Small:

Celebrate every milestone, achievement, and breakthrough along the way, no matter how small. Recognize and appreciate your progress, resilience, and hard work, and take pride in the journey you've embarked upon as a student entrepreneur. Each success, no matter how incremental, brings you closer to realizing your dreams.

Believe in Yourself and Your Potential:

Believe in yourself, your abilities, and your potential to achieve greatness. Have confidence in your ideas, skills, and capacity to overcome challenges and turn your vision into reality. Cultivate a growth mindset, embrace self-belief, and trust in your ability to succeed against all odds.

Keep Learning and Growing:

Never stop learning, growing, and expanding your horizons as an entrepreneur. Seek out opportunities for self-improvement, skill development, and personal growth. Embrace failure as a catalyst for learning, and continuously iterate, adapt, and innovate in pursuit of your goals.

Dream Big and Dare to Pursue Your Passions:

Dream big, think boldly, and dare to pursue your passions with unwavering determination and courage. Don't be afraid to take risks, challenge conventions, and pursue unconventional paths in pursuit of your entrepreneurial aspirations. Your dreams are valid, and with dedication and perseverance, they can become a reality.

Your Potential is Limitless:

Remember that your potential as a student entrepreneur is limitless. You have the power to create, innovate, and transform the world around you in ways you may have never imagined. Embrace the journey, embrace the challenges, and embrace the opportunities that lie ahead. Your future as an entrepreneur is bright, and the world is waiting for your unique talents and contributions.

As you embark on your entrepreneurial journey as a student, embrace the challenges, celebrate the victories, and stay true to your vision and values. With passion, perseverance, and a relentless pursuit of excellence, you have the power to create a future filled with success, fulfillment, and impact. Dream big, believe in yourself, and never stop striving for greatness. The world is yours to conquer, and your entrepreneurial journey has only just begun.

Final thoughts and call to action

As we come to the end of this journey exploring the world of student entrepreneurship, it's important to reflect on the valuable insights, strategies, and inspiration shared along the way. Whether you're just starting out on your entrepreneurial journey or already deep in the trenches of building your startup, remember that your potential as a student entrepreneur is boundless. Here are some final thoughts and a call to action to empower you to thrive:

Embrace the Journey: Entrepreneurship is a journey filled with twists, turns, and unexpected challenges. Embrace the journey with an open mind, a courageous spirit, and a relentless determination to overcome obstacles and seize opportunities along the way.

Persist Through Adversity: As a student entrepreneur, you will inevitably face setbacks, failures, and moments of doubt. Remember that adversity is an essential part of the entrepreneurial journey and an opportunity for growth and resilience. Stay persistent, stay resilient, and keep moving forward, no matter how tough the road may seem.

Seek Knowledge and Mentorship: Never stop seeking knowledge, learning from experiences, and seeking guidance from mentors and peers. Surround yourself with a supportive network of mentors, advisors, and fellow entrepreneurs who can offer insights, advice, and encouragement to help you navigate the challenges of entrepreneurship.

Take Action and Iterate: Don't wait for the perfect moment or the perfect plan to start taking action on your entrepreneurial ideas. Take bold, decisive action, and be willing to iterate, adapt, and pivot as you learn and grow along the way. Every step forward, no matter how small, brings you closer to your goals.

Stay True to Your Vision: Stay true to your vision, your values, and your purpose as you navigate the ups and downs of entrepreneurship.

Let your passion, your mission, and your values guide your decisions and actions, and never lose sight of the impact you aspire to create in the world.

Celebrate Your Successes: Celebrate every success, no matter how small, and acknowledge the progress you've made on your entrepreneurial journey. Take time to reflect on your achievements, express gratitude for the support of others, and celebrate the milestones you've reached along the way.

Pay It Forward: As you succeed and grow as a student entrepreneur, remember to pay it forward by supporting and empowering others on their entrepreneurial journeys. Share your knowledge, your experiences, and your resources with fellow students, aspiring entrepreneurs, and members of your community, and help create a culture of collaboration, innovation, and success.

Now, it's time for action. Take the lessons learned, the insights gained, and the inspiration found within these pages, and channel them into tangible actions that propel you forward on your entrepreneurial path. Whether it's refining your business idea, reaching out to potential mentors, or taking the first steps to launch your startup, the time to act is now.

Remember, the world needs your creativity, your innovation, and your entrepreneurial spirit now more than ever. So, dare to dream big, dare to take risks, and dare to make your mark on the world as a student entrepreneur. Your journey has the power to inspire, to transform, and to leave a lasting legacy for generations to come.

The future belongs to those who dare to imagine, to innovate, and to create. So, what are you waiting for? Your entrepreneurial journey awaits. Seize the opportunity, embrace the challenge, and embark on the adventure of a lifetime. The world is waiting for you to make your mark.

Appendix

Here are some worksheets, templates, and additional resources tailored for student entrepreneurs to streamline their planning, organization, and execution:

Business Plan Template:

Use a comprehensive business plan template to outline your business objectives, target market, value proposition, marketing strategy, financial projections, and more. This template can serve as a roadmap for your startup journey and help you communicate your vision to stakeholders. (Example: SCORE Business Plan Template)

SWOT Analysis Worksheet:

Conduct a SWOT analysis (Strengths, Weaknesses, Opportunities, Threats) to assess your startup's internal strengths and weaknesses as well as external opportunities and threats. This worksheet can help you identify key areas for strategic focus and action. (Example: MindTools SWOT Analysis Worksheet)

Financial Projections Spreadsheet:

Create a financial projections spreadsheet to forecast your startup's revenue, expenses, cash flow, and profitability over a specific period. This tool can help you estimate startup costs, track financial performance, and make informed decisions about budgeting and resource allocation. (Example: SCORE Financial Projections Template)

Marketing Plan Template:

Develop a comprehensive marketing plan template to outline your marketing objectives, target audience, channels, tactics, and metrics. This template can help you create a cohesive marketing strategy that effectively reaches and engages your customers. (Example: HubSpot Marketing Plan Template)

Pitch Deck Template:

Design a compelling pitch deck template to present your startup's vision, value proposition, market opportunity, product or service, business model, team, and financial projections to potential investors and stakeholders. This template can help you craft a persuasive and visually appealing presentation that captivates your audience. (Example: Canva Pitch Deck Templates)

Time Management Worksheet:

Utilize a time management worksheet to prioritize tasks, set deadlines, and allocate time effectively to academic studies, entrepreneurial activities, and personal commitments. This worksheet can help you optimize your productivity and balance competing priorities. (Example: Time Management Worksheet Template)

Networking Tracker Template:

Keep track of your networking activities, contacts, meetings, and follow-ups using a networking tracker template. This tool can help you build and nurture relationships with mentors, peers, investors, and industry professionals to support your entrepreneurial journey. (Example: Smartsheet Networking Tracker Template)

Goal Setting Worksheet:

Set SMART (Specific, Measurable, Achievable, Relevant, Time-bound) goals for your startup and personal development using a goal setting worksheet. This tool can help you clarify your objectives, track progress, and stay accountable to your aspirations. (Example: SMART Goals Worksheet Template)

Feedback Survey Template:

Gather feedback from customers, users, and stakeholders using a feedback survey template. This tool can help you collect valuable insights, identify areas for improvement, and refine your product or service based on user feedback. (Example: SurveyMonkey Feedback Survey Template)

Resource Library and Online Courses:

Explore online resources, courses, webinars, and tutorials offered by entrepreneurship organizations, universities, and industry experts to deepen your knowledge, skills, and expertise in entrepreneurship. Websites like Coursera, Udemy, and LinkedIn Learning offer a wide range of courses on topics such as startup strategy, business development, marketing, finance, and more.

These worksheets, templates, and additional resources are designed to support student entrepreneurs in planning, organizing, and executing their startup ventures with efficiency and effectiveness. Whether you're refining your business plan, managing your finances, or networking with potential partners, these tools can help you streamline your processes and achieve success on your entrepreneurial journey.

Glossary of key terms

Here's a glossary of key terms relevant to student entrepreneurship:

Entrepreneurship: The process of identifying, creating, and pursuing opportunities to start and grow a business venture, often involving innovation, risk-taking, and resource mobilization.

Startup: A newly established business venture, typically characterized by innovation, rapid growth potential, and scalability.

Business Plan: A formal document that outlines the goals, objectives, strategies, and financial projections of a business venture, serving as a roadmap for its development and operation.

Value Proposition: The unique benefit or value that a product or service offers to customers, distinguishing it from competitors and addressing their needs or pain points.

Minimum Viable Product (MVP): The simplest version of a product or service that allows a startup to test its core assumptions and gather feedback from early adopters before investing significant resources into development.

SWOT Analysis: A strategic planning tool used to assess a business's strengths, weaknesses, opportunities, and threats, helping to identify internal capabilities and external factors that may impact its success.

Pitch Deck: A presentation, typically consisting of slides, used by entrepreneurs to pitch their startup idea or business to potential investors, stakeholders, or partners.

Lean Startup: An approach to entrepreneurship that emphasizes rapid experimentation, iterative product development, and customer feedback to build and launch successful businesses with minimal resources.

Customer Relationship Management (CRM): A strategy and software system used to manage interactions and relationships with customers, including sales, marketing, and customer service activities.

Financial Projections: Forecasts and estimates of a business's future financial performance, including revenue, expenses, cash flow, and profitability, used for budgeting, planning, and decision-making.

Networking: Building and nurturing relationships with other entrepreneurs, investors, mentors, and industry professionals to gain support, advice, and opportunities for collaboration and growth.

Intellectual Property (IP): Legal rights granted to individuals or businesses to protect their inventions, creative works, and proprietary information, including patents, trademarks, copyrights, and trade secrets.

Bootstrapping: Funding a startup using personal savings, revenue generated from sales, or other low-cost methods, without relying on external investment or financing.

Venture Capital: Funding provided by venture capital firms or investors to startups and high-growth companies in exchange for equity ownership, typically used to accelerate growth and scale operations.

Angel Investor: An individual who provides financial backing and mentorship to startups and early-stage companies, often in exchange for equity ownership or convertible debt.

Accelerator: A program or organization that provides mentorship, resources, and networking opportunities to startups in exchange for equity, typically over a fixed period, to help them accelerate growth and scale.

Incubator: A program or organization that provides support, resources, and workspace to startups and early-stage companies, often focusing on nurturing and developing their ideas and business models.

Elevator Pitch: A brief and compelling summary of a startup idea or business, typically delivered in 30 seconds to two minutes, designed to quickly capture the attention of potential investors, customers, or partners.

Scaling: The process of expanding and growing a business to increase its market share, revenue, and profitability, and often involving the development of new products, markets, or distribution channels

Exit Strategy: A plan or strategy for how entrepreneurs and investors intend to exit or liquidate their investment in a startup, such as through acquisition, merger, IPO (Initial Public Offering), or other means.

Don't miss out!

Visit the website below and you can sign up to receive emails whenever Asit Saha publishes a new book. There's no charge and no obligation.

https://books2read.com/r/B-A-WRTEB-HOLAD

BOOKS 2 READ

Connecting independent readers to independent writers.

About the Author

Writes to motivate and entertain.